BRITTONS BOWRE OF DELIGHTS

BRITTONS BOWRE
OF DELIGHTS

1591

EDITED BY

HYDER EDWARD ROLLINS

NEW YORK / RUSSELL & RUSSELL

FIRST PUBLISHED IN 1933
REISSUED, 1968, BY RUSSELL & RUSSELL
A DIVISION OF ATHENEUM HOUSE, INC.
WITH THE PERMISSION OF
THE HENRY E. HUNTINGTON LIBRARY AND ART GALLERY
L. C. CATALOG CARD NO: 68-28742
PRINTED IN THE UNITED STATES OF AMERICA

CONTENTS

PHOTOGRAPHIC FACSIMILES

INTRODUCTION

INTRODUCTION

BRITTONS BOWRE OF DELIGHTS [1] is one of the most interesting poetical miscellanies of the Elizabethan period and one of the rarest books in the English language. Of the first edition (1591), which is here reproduced, the only known copy, inaccessible to students for many years, is now in the Huntington Library; of the second edition (1597) but two copies are extant, one in the Huntington Library, the other in the British Museum.

It is impossible to keep from sympathizing with that editor-of-all-work, Dr. Alexander B. Grosart, when he tells of his unsuccessful attempts to see and to secure permission to reprint the unique, or supposedly unique, Breton items once in the Britwell Library. In *The Works in Verse and Prose of Nicholas Breton* (2 volumes, 1875–1879) he necessarily omits his usual word *Complete*, and frequently he laments his hard luck. "I also poignantly regret," he writes in one place,[2] "the inaccessibility of the exemplars at Britwell of such of Breton's books as are nowhere else preserved"; "it makes me heart-sore not to be able to reproduce [them]," he adds in another;[3] and, finally, "No one either save myself can estimate the disappointment that I feel in being unable to 'complete' the Works by adding the FOUR [4]

---

[1] Merely for convenience this book is usually referred to in the following pages as *The Bower*.

[2] Grosart's Breton, I, xxv.   [3] *Ibid.*, p. lxxiii.

[4] These were (to use modernized titles) *The Works of a Young Wit* (1577), *The Bower* (1591), *Pasquil's Mistress* (1600), *Old Madcap's New Gallimaufry* (1602). Grosart might have added *The Arbor of Amorous Devices* (1597), since he followed a sorely mutilated and imperfect copy.

preserved in the famous library of BRITWELL. I trust some
after-comer may be fortunate enough to supplement my collection with these, either by access to those now withheld, or
by the discovery of other exemplars." [1] Grosart struggled
valiantly to make good the deficiencies of his edition by reprinting various manuscript copies of poems which he
guessed to be in *The Bower* and *The Arbor of Amorous Devices* (1597). But from that day to this almost nobody has
been permitted to see *The Bower*. The action of the Huntington Library trustees in sponsoring a facsimile edition is but
one of many proofs of the fact that England's loss is often
England's, as well as America's, gain.

The present facsimile reproduction is confined to the first
edition of 1591, so that a brief bibliographical description of
the 1597 edition is herewith added:

BRITTONS/ BOWRE OF/ Delights./ CONTAYN-
ING./ Many, moſt deleƈtable and/ fine deuiſes, of rare
Epitaphes, pleaſant Poems,/ Paſtoralls and Sonnets./ By
N. B. Gent./ [Device as in the 1591 edition.[2]] Imprinted at

----

[1] Grosart's Breton, I, lxxii.

[2] It represents, above the motto "DROIT ET LOYAL," a "standing
bear" chained with his paws on a tree-trunk, and is not mentioned in R. B.
McKerrow's *Printers' & Publishers' Devices in England & Scotland 1485-1640*
(1913), probably because it is rather a family crest than a printer's device. The
crest, or badge, and the motto belonged to the Earl of Leicester, and they appear
in the cut of his armorial bearings that adorns the versos of the title-pages in
William Morel's commentary on Latin verbs (1583) and Geoffrey Whitney's *A
Choice of Emblemes* (1586). The bear and ragged staff was likewise the badge
of the earls of Warwick (see Henry Green's discussion — of which Mr. F. B.
Williams reminded me — in his edition of Whitney [1866], pp. 314, 347). Hence
in the second part of *Henry VI*, V. i. 202-204, the Earl of Warwick says,

> "Now, by my father's badge, old Nevil's crest,
> The rampant bear chain'd to the ragged staff,
> This day I'll wear aloft my burgonet."

BRITTONS
BOWRE OF
Delights.

CONTAYNING,

Many, moſt delectable and
fine deuiſes, of rare Epitaphes, pleaſant Poems,
Paſtoralls and Sonnets.

By N.B. Gent,

Imprinted at London by Richard Iohnes, at the Roſe
and Crowne, neere Saint Andrewes Church
in Holborne, 1597.

Title-page of *Brittons Bowre of Delights* 1597

*L*ondon by Richard Iohnes, at the Roſe/ and Crowne, neere Saint Andrewes Church/ in Holborne. 1597./

Collation: 4°, sigs. A–F⁴, unpaged. [A1] title; verso blank: [A2] "To the Gentlemen/ Readers" (in italic and roman type); verso with the demi-lion rampant reproduced facing p. xii: A3-[F4ᵛ] text of the poems, in roman and occasional italic type, with "*F*/*N*/*S*. N. ʙ. *Gent.*", followed by a type-ornament at the foot of [F4ᵛ].

Running-titles: A3ᵛ–B4ᵛ, "AMORIS LACHRIMAE" (followed by a comma on the verso of A3, apparently by a period on the other versos and on the rectos); D2ᵛ–D4ᵛ, "BRITTONS VISION."; E1–E2, "BRITTONS DREAME." The other rectos have "POEMS AND SONETS." C1, "PASTORALS AND SONETS." C2 to D2, E3 to F4; the other versos, "PLEASANT POEMS," C1ᵛ to D1ᵛ, E2ᵛ to F4ᵛ (misprinted "PLEAS*A*N" on E4ᵛ). In nearly all the running-titles wrong-font letters, especially italic, appear, and the punctuation-marks are badly blurred.

Signatures: Signed in threes except, of course, for A1 and A2. Signature E1 is misprinted "F."; B2 and F2 are followed by commas instead of periods.

Catch-words: If is misprinted on C3ᵛ for *In*, *An* on E3ᵛ for *And*. All the other catch-words (each is in roman or italic type) appear to be correct, though several (A4, B4ᵛ, C1, C2ᵛ, D1ᵛ, E3) are so blurred as to be illegible, and *The* (B3ᵛ) has its initial letter out of alignment.

In the following pages this 1597 edition is assumed to be the second, but of course other editions may have been published between 1591 and 1597 without leaving a trace. The separate texts of the 1597 edition are fully collated in the Notes with those of the 1591 edition, so that it has seemed unnecessary to reproduce the former entire.

Halliwell-Phillipps, in his folio Shakespeare (XI [1863], 204) comments on the foregoing lines: "The ancient badge of the Warwick family, said to be in allusion to the name of the founder of the family in England, Urso de Abitot."

For *Brittons Bowre of Delights* we are indebted to the enterprise of a none too scrupulous printer, Richard Jones. He had been admitted to the Stationers' Company on August 7, 1564, registering a ballad in 1564–1565 as his first work.[1] Throughout his life he specialized in ballads, 123 being entered by him on August 8, 1586; but he also printed or published some ninety books, among them certain works of George Whetstone, Thomas Lodge, Thomas Nashe, and Christopher Marlowe. Occasionally his enterprise led to trouble; as when in June and August, 1579,[2] he was fined for disorderly printing, and when on January 21, 1583,[3] for a similar offense the Stationers' Company ordered him to be fined and imprisoned. Dr. R. B. McKerrow,[4] however, believes that Jones was "on the whole . . . an orderly member" of the company, in which he spent thirty-eight years of business life, making his last entry of a book on June 4, 1602.

Jones had a fondness for poetical miscellanies. His most successful venture of that kind was *A Handful of Pleasant Delights*, originally issued in 1566,[5] but surviving in one imperfect copy dated 1584. Less successful, though far more pretentious, was *A Gorgeous Gallery of Gallant Inventions*, which he published in 1578. Again, in 1575 he issued a tiny book, *A Small Handful of Fragrant Flowers*, under the initials *N. B.*, with the result that it is still often wrongly attributed to Breton. But his relations with Breton were obviously cordial, since he printed that poet's *A Flourish upon Fancy* in

[1] Arber's *Transcript of the Registers of the Company of Stationers of London*, I [1875], 271, 278.
[2] *Ibid.*, II, 849–850.
[3] *Ibid.*, p. 853.
[4] *A Dictionary of Printers and Booksellers*, 1910, p. 159.
[5] See my note in *Modern Language Notes*, XLI (1926), 327.

Device from *Brittons Bowre of Delights* 1597 A2ᵛ

1577 and 1582, and registered for publication on September 9, 1578, Breton's *The Pain of Pleasure*, a work now unknown.

On May 3, 1591, Jones "Entred for his Copie in full Court Brytons *Bow[e]rs of Delightes* beinge vnder th[e h]and of master Mathew Heton." [1] Publication of the book in 1591 saved a number of poems from total extinction, and gave the earliest texts of various others. Now Richard Tottel had set the fashion for prefaces with the few prose lines he contributed to the famous *Songs and Sonnets* of 1557, and Jones whole-heartedly adopted it. For *A Handful* he wrote doggerel verses called "The Printer to the Reader." For *The Bower* and *The Arbor of Amorous Devices* he penned long addresses to "the gentlemen readers"; and by the time he got to R. S.'s *Phillis and Flora* (1598) the habit was so fixed that he began his preface, "Courtuous Gentlemen, according to my accustomed maner, which is, to acquaint you with any Booke, or matter I print."

Jones informs his gentlemanly readers that *The Bower* was printed "in the Authours absence" and that faults, like misprints, are due to his own negligence, not to "any ignorance in the Author." Indirectly he shows beyond question that the book is a publication made without the knowledge of the author, or authors. "I am (onely) the Printer of them, chiefly to pleasure you, and partly to profit my selfe," he asserts. But it is practically certain that Jones was compiler and editor as well, and that he made "improvements" in the texts. Such was his custom in dealing even with the greatest writers. So he tells the readers of Marlowe's *Tamburlaine* (1592) about his editorial activities: "I have purposely

[1] Arber's *Transcript*, II, 581.

omitted and left out some fond and frivolous gestures, digressing, and, in my poor opinion, far unmeet for the matter," although on the stage they were "greatly gaped at" by the ignorant playgoers. Still another publication, *The English Courtier, and the Cutrey-gentleman* (1586), he dedicates to Sir Francis Walsingham, with the artless comment that the anonymous author did not wish to see his work printed, much less dedicated to that distinguished statesman. "Notwithstanding, without his leaue, I make bolde to aduenture the one and the other."

Evidently Jones put Breton's name on the title-page to attract buyers. In this action there was nothing especially discreditable; or, at any rate, various printers before as well as after 1591 indulged in the same practise with other popular writers, Shakespeare among them. It seems credible, too, that in putting Breton's name in large type on the title-page Jones did not intend to father all the poems on him. One poem, indeed (No. 40), he signed with the initials of its real author, the seventeenth Earl of Oxford. Fortunately, Breton gave his own views of the matter, vigorously denouncing Jones for publishing the compositions of other writers under the name *Britton*, but showing no especial indignation or surprise at finding some of his own poems published without his knowledge or consent. He felt as indignant as Shakespeare later did (if Thomas Heywood may be believed) when William Jaggard printed under the name *Shakespeare* verses of Heywood and others in *The Passionate Pilgrim* (1599, 1612).

In *The Pilgrimage To Paradise, Ioyned With The Countesse of Penbrookes loue* (1592) Breton emphatically voices his opinions. His preface "To the Gentlemen students and Scholers of Oxforde," dated April 12, is followed at the bottom of the page [1] by the note:

Gentlemen there hath beene of late printed in london by one Richarde Ioanes, a printer, a booke of english verses, entituled *Bretons bower of delights*: I protest it was donne altogether without my consent or knowledge, & many thinges of other mens mingled with few of mine, for except *Amoris Lachrimæ*: an epitaphe vpon Sir Phillip Sydney, and one or two other toies, which I know not how he vnhappily came by, I haue no part with any of thē: and so I beseech yee assuredly beleeue.

To this protest Jones paid no heed. Only two years later [2] he impudently issued *The Arbor of Amorous Devices* with Breton's name on the title-page, but in the preface he frankly admitted that the book is a miscellany containing "many mens workes excellent Poets, and most, not the meanest in estate and degree." Here he included ten poems which he had already printed in *The Bower*; and he issued new editions of both *The Bower* and *The Arbor*, still under Breton's name, in 1597. It is a noteworthy fact that Breton later on chose Jones as the publisher for a new book, *Old Madcap's New Gallimaufry*, in 1602. Evidently the dispute between the poet and his printer had an amicable ending.

[1] John Wolf registered *The Pilgrymage to Paradise*, with no author's name, on January 23, 1591; that is, more than three months before *The Bower* was licensed — a not wholly clear fact. In the printed edition of *The Pilgrimage*, however (assuming that it *was* the subject of Wolf's entry), Breton's disclaimer appears to be an afterthought to his formal preface. Perhaps attention should be called here to Charles Crawford's assertion (*Studies in Philology*, extra series, I [1929], 7) that, because Breton "had had a tiff with his printer, Richard Jones, he disowned his *Bowre of Delights*, and wished readers to believe that Jones had obtained it in a manner unknown to him, and falsely assigned the work to him, his share in it being but small."

[2] As I shall show in my introduction to *The Arbor*, though only an edition of 1597 has been preserved.

The first edition of *The Bower* contains 56 poems, the second 41, Nos. 6–20 being omitted. These omissions were supposed by early scholars to have been made as a concession to Breton's protest. W. C. Hazlitt,[1] for example, describes *The Bower* of 1597 as a new edition "with many alterations introduced, no doubt at the author's desire, perhaps under his eye." But the facts are otherwise. What happened was that *The Phoenix Nest* appeared late in 1593 while Jones was compiling *The Arbor of Amorous Devices*, and made public property of a number of lyrics that he had intended to print, so that in his preface to *The Arbor* he regretfully admits: "had not the Phenix preuented me of some the best stuffe she furnisht her nest with of late: this *Arbor* had bin somewhat the more[2] handsomer trimmed vp, beside a larger scope for gentlemen to recreate them selues." Finding himself fore-stalled, Jones discarded the poems which *The Phoenix Nest* had used, and in order to make *The Arbor* of proper size he transferred to the end of it ten poems (Nos. 11–20)[3] that he had already printed in *The Bower*. Then in 1597 he reissued both *The Bower* and *The Arbor*: perhaps the latter was printed first, as in the former he omitted Nos. 11–20. Why he excluded Nos. 6–9 from the second editions of these two books is by no means clear, but it hardly seems likely that Breton's protest was responsible. I suppose that No. 10 was dropped because it had been included in *The Phoenix Nest*,

---

[1] *Hand-book to the Popular . . . Literature*, 1867, p. 56. He also says that the Farmer copy sold in 1798 for £1. 13s. See *Bibliotheca Farmeriana*, 1798, lot 6395.

[2] Misprinted *mote*.

[3] They are Nos. 35–44 in *The Arbor* of 1597, and it is almost certain that they had a similar position in the lost first edition.

and because it was everywhere assumed to have been composed not by Breton but by Sir Walter Raleigh.

In reissuing *The Bower* Jones made no alterations in his
preface by way of reply to Breton, unless he had the poet in
mind when he substituted "if you happen iustlie to finde any
fault" for "where you happen to find any fault." In both
prefaces "the Author" is mentioned, in spite of the fact that
No. 40 is signed with the initials of the Earl of Oxford. Jones
was extremely careless about attributions of authorship in
his other miscellanies, like *A Handful of Pleasant Delights*
and *A Gorgeous Gallery of Gallant Inventions*. Perhaps he did
not know the real authors of all the poems that he included
in *The Bower*; for surely it would have added to the popular-
ity, or rather to the salability, of the book to have given the
names of several well-known authors instead of only one —
to have issued it as a genuine miscellany, like Tottel's, not as
the work of a single author. If he did not know the authors'
names, Jones was faced with the alternative of lumping the
anonymous poems under *Britton* or else, again like Tottel's
Miscellany, under *uncertain authors*. From the point of view
of salesmanship it was undoubtedly wise to choose *Britton*.

These speculations are countenanced by a number of mis-
leading signatures which Jones (or his "corrector of the
press") did insert. Wherever he observed acrostics in the
poems (and he overlooked several striking cases), he usually
not only emphasized the acrostic by inserting extra initial
letters in roman type but he also added a "finis" followed by
the initials or the name thus designated, though not at No.
43. For instance No. 2, the initial letters of which spell
"Anne Parker," is signed "Finis. A. P.", and in the same

fashion Nos. 3 and 4 are attributed to "Trentame" and "Garet." But the verses in question were unmistakably written about, not by, the ladies whose names are played upon. Certain authors' names, however, could properly have been introduced. The Earl of Oxford wrote not merely No. 40, as Jones indicates, but also No. 54 and possibly No. 3. Sir Walter Raleigh was probably the author of Nos. 10 and 48 and, less probably, No. 14. Furthermore, No. 51 is a condensed version of a well-known lyric, in Tottel's *Miscellany*, by the Earl of Surrey. Most people in 1591 would doubtless have assumed that Sir Philip Sidney composed No. 8.

Nicholas Breton himself unquestionably wrote most of the poems, although his animus against Jones made him acknowledge the authorship of No. 1 and "one or two other toys" only. The similarity in diction, subject-matter, and technique of the majority of the fifty-six poems is very noticeable — the use of favorite words like *angels, bower, dainty, favor, feature, heavenly, heavens, saint, sweet,* the dependence on abstractions (often arranged in pairs) like *Virtue and Honor, Love and Beauty, Wit and Will,* the continual feminine rimes like *bereft me: left me.* Such resemblances imply that Breton's share in *The Bower* was large, and one student [1] finds that "no less than twenty-six poems . . . afford some evidence of Breton's authorship." At any rate, up to the present day the poet's reputation has depended to a great extent on *The Bower* and *The Arbor,* the separate poems in which, even when no irrefutable proof of their authorship is forthcoming, have usually been attributed to him

[1] F. H. McCloskey, *Studies in the Works of Nicholas Breton,* p. 331 (Harvard Ph.D. thesis, 1929). He particularizes Nos. 5-7, 12, 15, 17-21, 23-30, 36, 37, 39, 41, 47, 50, 55, 56.

and often lavishly praised. Thus Sir Egerton Brydges and Joseph Haslewood, editing *England's Helicon* in 1812,[1] maintained that the genius of Thomas Lodge and of Breton "was not only elegant and highly-polished, but pure, unsophisticated, and far above the taste of their age"; that if Breton "possessed less sentiment than Lodge, perhaps his fancy was still more delicate and playful, and his expression not less simple and harmonious"; and that No. 5 "is a little finished gem, exquisitely tender and chaste." Sir Sidney Lee, writing on Sidney in the *Dictionary of National Biography*, went so far as to call No. 1 "a charming elegy," though it is not likely that anyone else will agree with that characterization. On the whole, the poems are stiff, artificial, and "conceited," with a profusion of unfortunate figures like "Handes sawe the price" (49.26). They have, nevertheless, many points of interest for the scholar, and their quaintness may appeal to merely casual readers.

In his preface Jones expressed the hope that the gentlemen readers will like the poems especially "for the Subiet and worthinesse of the persons they doo concerne." Or, in other words, he suggests that his book is largely a miscellany of verses by and about courtiers and court-ladies. The most important name connected with it is, of course, that of Sir Philip Sidney, in whose memory is written the first and by far the longest poem, Breton's "Amoris Lachrimae" (No. 1), as well as five other shorter poems (Nos. 18, 19, 28–30). Queerly enough, however, although the initial letters of Nos. 28–30 spell "Philip Philip," "Philip," and "Philip Sidney," Jones did not emphasize these acrostics typographically, though he

[1] Pp. v, vii, xx.

did so in the 1597 edition. No doubt during his first printing he failed to see them.

An identical lack of editorial care is to be detected elsewhere. Thus No. 8 spells the acrostic "Penelope Rich," a fact that would very likely have suggested Sidney's authorship in 1591; but Jones (and some modern readers, like Grosart) failed to observe it. In the same way No. 34 was written to celebrate "Frauncis Haward" (or Howard), but Jones, not noticing the acrostic, gave it the stupid title "In commendation of the maides of Honour." Manifestly the author wrote "In Commendation of the [or a] Maid of Honor." Four other poems (Nos. 2–4, 43) commend ladies — Anne Parker, Elizabeth Trentham, Elizabeth Garret, and Anne Hopton — and by not stressing the tributes to Lady Rich and Lady Howard the printer made a grave mistake. That poems of this sort were acceptable and salable becomes evident when one finds Jones inserting in *The Arbor* new acrostic-verses on still other maids of honor.

The miscellany is only further proof of the looseness with which the word *sonnet* was employed in Elizabethan times. On the title-page and in the preface to *A Handful of Pleasant Delights* (1584) Jones uses *sonnets* as a synonym for *songs*, and his book contains no sonnets at all, in the modern meaning of that term. It happens that *The Bower* actually does have six regular English, or Shakespearean, sonnets (Nos. 10, 11, 16, 21, 22, 34); but, significantly enough, to none of these is the term *sonnet* applied.[1] Jones, however, uses *sonnet* ten times: five times to describe poems in six-line

---

[1] Nor is it applied to the three Shakespearean sonnets (Nos. 29, 35, 40) in *The Arbor*, where, indeed, the word is not used at all.

stanzas (Nos. 14, 41, 42, 45, 54), four times to describe poems in four-line stanzas (Nos. 33, 44, 48, 52), once for a fourteen-line poem in poulter's measure (No. 6). This last occurrence plainly has no significance, for Nos. 7 and 40, which are identical in length and meter with No. 6, are not called sonnets. To Jones and to nearly all other Elizabethans up to 1591 *sonnet* and *lyric* and *song* were convenient synonyms.

With similar looseness he employs the term *pastoral*, which is meaningless as applied in the titles of Nos. 5, 9, 15, and 46. But one must not be too finicky, for various modern printers and scholars indulge in phraseology equally vague. To illustrate, the Spiral Press of New York in 1927 issued a pretty little book called *Phillida and Coridon and Other Pastorals by Nicholas Breton*, which includes twelve "pastorals," four of them being from *The Bower* (Nos. 5, 15, 47, 50). Perhaps Jones, no less than his modern followers, considered the mere mention of Phyllis or Corydon sufficient to transform a simple lyric into a pastoral.

The vocabulary of *The Bower* affords some interesting words and usages that deserve mention. Thus *wonder-stone* (25.24) does not appear in *A New English Dictionary*. Earlier than any examples listed in that work are *at beck and bay* (1593) at 59.17, *bleeding*, full of anguish (1596), at 25.9, *level*, to aim (1592), at 10.6, *mouldy chaps* (1595) at 40.9, *over-gazed* (1600) at 49.16, and the participial adjective *sorrowed*, sorrowful (1607), at 39.6. To the uses cited in the dictionary one might profitably add *admire*, to wonder at (24.4), *all amort*, dejectedly (13.9, 26.32), *blows*, blowzes, coarse country wenches (33.9). The dictionary gives no instances between 1530 and

1667 of the adverbial phrase *to bedward* (50.5); of the present participle *blaying*, bleating (13.30), between 1581 and 1617; of *bunting* (41.27) between 1440 and 1601; of *cavaliroes*, cavaliers or horse-soldiers (43.31), between 1470 and 1598; of *cavillers* (3.20) between 1574 and 1667; of *findfaults* (3.20) between 1577 and 1656; of *harp upon* (11.32) between 1562 and 1602; of *Ohone*, a ballad tune (36.2), between 1480 and 1604; of *recording*, singing (18.14), between 1530 and 1611. Attention might be called, also, to the frequent proverbs and proverbial phrases; as "a little was a feast" (8.8), "words are wind" (11.25), "fools have long coats and monkeys have no breeches" (34.32), "find the fox before you begin the chase" (35.8), "shut not a rat within a sugar-hutch" (35.9), "seek not a woodcock in a swallow's nest" (35.12), "to think one blind when one did only wink" (37.24), "who is so blind as they that will not see" (41.7), "a bunting can't beget a lark" (41.27), "*in anno* out of mind" (42.4), "silence seldom serves a lover" (46.32), "labor in vain" (49.4), "who deals with fire may burn his fingers" (50.10), "a friend is best proved in need" (56.17).

The meters in *The Bower* are worthy of some notice. The Shakespearean and poulter's-measure sonnets, already referred to, made their appearance just when the real vogue of the sonnet, a form neglected for years after its introduction in 1557, was beginning. The two pretty ballads (Nos. 33, 49) may have found their way into the book from broadsides published earlier by Jones, and No. 15 was frequently issued (without Breton's name) as a broadside ballad in the seventeenth century. Old-fashioned taste is evidenced by Nos. 5, 18, 20, 46, which (like Nos. 6, 7, 40) are written in poulter's measure. But no less than twenty-three poems are in the six-line iambic pentameter stanza, riming *ababcc*, familiar because of its adoption by Shakespeare for *Venus and Adonis*. Iambic pentameter quatrains appear four times,[1] octameter couplets twice,[2] trochaic tetrameter once.[3] *The Bower*, then, is "miscellaneous" in its meters no less than in its contributors.

So far as is known, all but two poems (Nos. 40, 54) were printed for the first time in *The Bower*, Nos. 8 and 9 are to be found only in its pages, and many others occur only here in printed (not manuscript) form. Here, too, are the earliest texts of Nos. 10, 14, 48, poems which, along with part of No. 23, were included two years later in R. S.'s *The Phoenix Nest* (1593). On the title-page that miscellany professes to be "Built vp with the most rare and refined workes. . . . Neuer before this time published." R. S. may not have known *The Bower*, or he may have ignored it as an unauthorized publication, since his own was (there is good reason to believe) based upon holograph texts furnished him by the authors, one of whom was Nicholas Breton. As is pointed out in the Notes, later copies of the *Bower* poems are fairly common. Especially numerous are the texts given in MS. Additional 34064. The British Museum catalogue describes the manuscript as having been written in the late sixteenth and early seventeenth centuries. It belonged in 1596 to Anthony Babington, of Warrington, and a little later to a Henry and a Roger Wright. While in the hands of F. W. Cosens it was studied and much of its contents printed by Grosart in his edition of Breton, after which it came into the possession of

---

[1] Nos. 8, 12, 13, 25.   [2] Nos. 27, 32.   [3] No. 15.

the British Museum on June 15, 1891. Grosart placed great
faith in this manuscript; but, as its Breton poems were certainly copied from print (many of them from *The Bower* of
1597), its texts in themselves are of no special value.

There are various signs that *The Bower* was a popular
book. For one thing it reached at least a second edition in
six years' time; for another, four of its poems (Nos. 5, 15, 47,
50) were taken over by *England's Helicon*, 1600, where the
pastoral note made them appropriate, and where, on the
strength of Jones's title-page, they were signed with Breton's
name. Again, Thomas Heywood admired No. 46 so much
that he rewrote it as a song for his play, *The Fair Maid of the
Exchange* (1607). Years later, in 1639, Samuel Pick bor-
rowed Nos. 15, 31, and 54 for inclusion as his own verses in
Festum Voluptatis; Or, The Banquet of Pleasure. In company with *The Arbor*, *The Bower* helped Breton attain his
place of high distinction in Elizabethan critical works, so
that Francis Meres, in *Palladis Tamia* (1598), classed him
as one of the best English lyric poets along with Daniel,
Drayton, Spenser, and Shakespeare. On the contrary, the
first definite reference to *The Bower* is distinctly and unwar-
rantably hostile: Thomas Nashe, in his introduction to Sidney's *Astrophel and Stella*, 1591, remarks, "Gentlemen . . .
that haue seene *Pan* sitting in his bower of delights, & a number of *Midasses* to admire his miserable hornepipes, let not
your surfeted sight, new come frō such puppet play, think
scorne to turn aside into this Theater of pleasure." [1]

The Bower quickly vanished from sight in the seventeenth
century, perhaps because most of the copies had been liter-

---

[1] See also the notes to 12.10.

ally read out of existence. The unique copy now known remained securely hidden from most students until it took its
final journey — to California. No reference is made to *The
Bower* in Edward Phillips's *Theatrum Poetarum* (1675) or in
Bishop Percy's *Reliques of Ancient English Poetry* (1765),
though the latter work pays some slight attention to Breton
himself.[1] It was unknown to George Ellis when in his *Speci-
mens of the Early English Poets* (1790) he reprinted three of
Breton's poems from *England's Helicon*. In his 1801 edition
Ellis included eight poems under Breton's and one under the
Earl of Oxford's name, two of them (Nos. 32 and 40)[2] perhaps
from *The Bower* of 1597, which is mentioned in his editions
of 1801 and 1803. Joseph Ritson, in *Bibliographia Poetica*,
1802, likewise refers only to the 1597 edition; Sir Egerton
Brydges, editing Phillips's *Theatrum* in 1800, as well as *Ex-
cerpta Tudoriana* in 1814, apparently did not even know *The
Bower* by title, nor did Thomas Campbell, the editor of *Speci-
mens of the British Poets* (1819).

Meanwhile the unique copy of the 1591 *Bower* had frequently changed owners. From the James Perry collection it
went to Richard Heber for £26. 15s. 6d. in 1822; at Heber's
sale in 1834 it was bought by Thomas Jolley for £16. 5s.;
after Jolley's death it was sold to W. H. Christie-Miller in
1843 for £31; and it remained in the Britwell Library of the
Millers until in 1922 it was purchased by the Rosenbach
Company for £755,[3] from whom it came to Mr. Huntington.

[1] Percy reprinted Nos. 5 and 40 from other sources.
[2] II, 139–140, 256–258.
[3] See Sotheby's catalogue of the S. R. Christie-Miller sale, February 6, 1922,
lot 73, and *Book-Prices Current*, XXXVI (1922), 120. It is described as having
"some lower margins cropped and some signatures and catch-words cut into."

A like fate overtook one copy of the 1597 edition. Once owned by the famous seventeenth-century antiquary and diarist, Narcissus Luttrell, it passed through the hands of George Ellis and Richard Heber into the British Museum. The second copy, along with other treasures (all in perfect condition), was discovered on September 23, 1867, by Charles Edmonds in a disused lumber-room at Lamport Hall, Northamptonshire, the seat of Sir Charles Edmund Isham. From Lamport it went to Britwell Court, whence at the Christie-Miller sale on December 16, 1919,[1] it was bought by Mr. George D. Smith for Mr. Huntington.

So rare, so interesting, and so pleasing a book as *Brittons Bowre of Delights* deserves to be better known.

[1] See Sotheby's sale-catalogue of that date, lot 10, and *Book-Prices Current*, XXXIV (1920), 110, where the price paid is recorded as £440.

BRITTONS BOWRE OF DELIGHTS

BRITTONS
BOWRE OF
Delights.

CONTAYNING

Many, moſt delectable and fine deuices,
of rare Epitaphes, pleaſant Poems, Paſto-
rals and Sonets

By N. B. Gent.

DROIT · ET · LOYAL

Imprinted at London by Richard Ihones, at the
Roſe and Crowne neere Holborne
Bridge. 1591.

To the Gentlemen
Readers.

GENTLEMEN: I prefent you here, in the Authours abfence, with fundrie fine Deuices, and rare conceytes, in Englifh verfe: by the names of Epitaphes, Poems, Paftorals and Sonets: fome of worthines, and fome of wantonnes, yet (all in my poore cenfure) wittie, pleafant, & commendable: It any like you, (as I hope they wil) partly, for the well penning of them: but fpecially, for the Subiet and worthineffe of the perfons they doo concerne) though (happly) you efteeme the reft ot leffe regard: I then haue my defire, and count my labour and charges well beftowed. I am (onely) the Printer of them, chiefly to pleafure you, and partly to profit my felfe, if they prooue to your good liking: if otherwife, my hope is fruftrate, my labour loft, and all my coft is caft away. Pardon mee, (good Gentlemen) of my prefumption, & protect me, I pray you, againft thofe Cauellers, and findfaults, that neuer like of any thing that they fee printed, though it be neuer fo wel compiled. And where you happen to find any fault, impute it to bee committed by the Printers negligence, then (otherwife) by any ignorance in the Author: and efpecially in A 3, about the middeft of the page, for lime oʒ lead, I pray you read it lime oʒ lead. So fhall your poore Printer haue iuft caufe hereafter to be more carefull, and acknowledge himfelfe moft bounden (at all times) to do you feruice to the vtmoft of his power,

[5]

[10]

[15]

[20]

[25]

[30]

Yours, R, I, Printer,

3

(1)   *Amoris Lachrimae.*
        A most singular and sweete Discourse of
            the life and death of S.P.S. Knight.

Among the woes of those vnhappie wights,
That haue set downe the sorrowes of their time,
Whose liues are most deuoid of al delights
And passe in griefe the pleasures of their prime:
  Let me discourse the secrets of my care,
  More then conceyte of sorrow can declare.

Some loose their wealth, it is a slender losse,
My life hath lost the treasure of my trust:
Some loose their health, alas a common crosse,
My lifes delight is buried in the dust:
  Some loose their friendes, it is no one mans woe,
  I lost a friend, such one there are no moe.

Some loose their loue, a sorrow neere the heart,
In kinde affect the crosse of onely crosses:
Some loose their liues, where sorrowes neuer part,
Some loose themselues in thinking of their losses:
  More then my selfe is such a friend bereft me,
  All wealth, nor health, nor loue, nor life hath left me.

And shall I tell what kinde of man he was,
Whome thus I lou'de: and neuer creature hated,
Imagine first it dooth my reason passe,
To write of him whome hiest power created:

For euerie part that vertue had desired,
Ioy of the heauens, and of the world admired.

Yet as my heart for griefe and sorrow can,
I will describe the substance of his state,
In childish yeares he was esteemed a man,
And halfe a man, more halfe a magistrate,
  On whome the Arts and Rules so attended,
  As all, in all, for all, he was commended.

Whose wisdome was not seene in wanton toies,
And though a wanton, yet not deuoid of wit,
Of worldly ieasts he neuer made his ioies,
Although sometimes he had a taste of it:
  For let the best that liues do what he can,
  In some things yet he shewes himself a man.

But if on earth there were a man deuine,
For Natures gifts and Vertues secret grace,
Then giue me leaue to say this loue of mine,
Was here too good to haue a dwelling place,
  But liues in heauen some high Angels office,
  Where God himselfe dooth vse him in his seruice.

To say yet more what (in effect) he was,
Let this suffice, in summe he was a man,
Whose heauenly wisedome found the way to passe,
More then the power of Wit and Reason can:
  In whose attempts the world thus well did know him,
  Nothing but death could euer ouerthrow him.

Comely of shape, and of a manly face,
Noble in birth, and of a princely minde,
Kinde in effect and of a courtly grace,
Courteous to all, and carefull of the kinde:
  Valure and Vertue, Learning, Bountie, Loue,
  These were the parts that did his honour proue.

Whose full perfection thus hath wisedome peased,
His wordes were substance, and his deeds diuine,
Reason the ground whereon his hope were raysed,
Labour his life, and Learning was his line:
　Truth was his loue, and Triall his intent,
　Care his conceipt, and Honour his content.

He spake no worde, but carried full his waight,
He nothing did that euer tooke disgrace,
He had no minde to muse vpon deceyte,
He built in heauen his onely byding place.
　He lou'd the Church where Saints do build the steeple.
　And sought the worlde where Angels are the people.

He trauaild farre when he was neerest home,
Where was no earth he could behold a land,
He sawe a house without care, lime or lome,
And saild the seas where there was neuer sand.
　He sounded depths, without eare lime or lead,
　And found out life, where other men were dead.

He fearde no foe, nor euer sought a friend,
He knew no want, and made no care of wealth,
He nought begun, but had a care to end,
And neuer lou'd the honour had in stealth:
　By fire and sword he wonne his worthy fame,
　That hath aduaunc'd the honour of his name.

In all the skie he honoured but a starre,
That was his course of all his kind affection,
Whose flame was nere, although the fire a farre,
Gatte him the light of loues direction:
　He was so kind and constant where he loued,
　As once resolu'd, he could not be remoued.

His hands was free to helpe the needie hart,
His heart was franke to fill the emptie hand,
His most desire was to reward desart,

And holde vp state where honour could not stande:
　His onely ioy was honour of the fielde,
　To conquere men, and make the Captaines yeelde.

Much was his care, and of his Countrey most,
Little his ioy, and in himselfe the least,
All for his friend, did seeme but little cost,
Yet to himselfe a little was a feast.
　High was their happe that might but be about him.
　Death is their life that mourne, to be without him.

Nowe iudge the life in leauing such a ioy,
The death in losse of such a daintie friend,
What may remoue the roote of this annoy,
Or howe this griefe may euer haue an ende.
　And if it be a care incurable,
　Thinke of the death where it is durable.

To liue in death is but a dying life,
To die in life, is but a liuing death,
Betwixt these two is such a deadly strife,
As make me draw this melancholike breath:
　Wherein conceite dooth liue so discontented,
　As neuer heart was euer so tormented.

A torment onely made but for the minde,
A minde ordainde but onely to distresse,
And such distresse as can no comfort finde,
But leaues the heart to die remedilesse:
　And such a death as liueth to beholde,
　Ten thousand torments more then can be tolde.

Yet through my penne can neuer halfe expresse,
The hideous torments of my heauie heart,
Let me set downe some touch of my distresse,
That some poore soule may helpe to beare a part:
　That in extremities when we are wo begon us,

8

The worlde may weepe to sit and looke vpon us.

Nature and Art are got about his graue,
And there sit wailing of each others losse,
Hard by the tombe sittes Sorrow in her caue,
Cutting her heart to thinke on honours crosse:
  And Wisedome weeping, wringing of her hands,
  To see the worlde in what a case it stands.

In this darke hole of death and heauinesse,
Sits wofull Bewtie with her blubbred eyes,
By her sits Loue, with Care all comfortlesse,
Recording of his mothers miseries:
  Among the rest that wailes the losse of friends,
  Sits Patience pricking of her fingers ends.

From Pities face doo fall the trickling teares,
Of torments such as teare the heart of Loue,
The Muses sit and rend their shriueled heares,
To see the paine that Loue and Bewtie proue.
  Among them all howe I am torne in sunder,
  And yet do liue, confesse it is a wonder.

I liue, oh liue, alas, I liue indeede,
But such a life was neuer such a death,
While fainting heart is but constrainde to feede,
Vpon the care of a consuming breath:
  O my sweete Muse, that knowest how I am vexed,
  Paint but one passion how I am perplexed.

I call for death, but yet he will not heare me,
I read my death, and rue my destinie,
I see my death, but he will not come neare me,
I feele my death, but yet I cannot die:
  But where nor death will kill, nor griefe be cured,
  Thinke what a death of deathes I haue endured.

Yet while I liue in all this miserie,
Let me go quarrell with this cruell fate,
Why death should do so great an iniurie,
Vnto the stay of such a happie state:
  At liuing things to make his Ieuell so,
  To kill a Phoenix when there were no mo.

Oh cruell Death what led thy hand awrie,
To take the best and leaue the worst behind,
To youth thou art vntimely destinie,
Thou mightest haue bene a comfort to the blind:
  And end the aged of their wearie time,
  And not a youth in pride of all his prime.

Thou moughtest haue shot at such a wretched thought,
As had past ouer all his pleasant yeares,
And killed the heart that is consumed to nought,
Which being tangled in these worldly briers,
  But Bewties loue, and Honors hart to bleed,
  Fie on thee death, it is too fowle a deed.

But well, the world will curse thee to thy face,
Bewtie and Loue will to the teeth defie thee,
Honor and Learning draw thee in disgrace,
Where no good thought shall euer once come nie thee:
  And for my selfe to see thee wo begone thee,
  Will pray to God all plagues may light vpon thee.

For I haue lost the honour of my loue,
My loue hath lost the honour of my life,
My life and loue doth such a passion proue,
As in the world was neuer such a strife:
  Where secret death and sorow are consented,
  To see the terror of a heart tormented.

Thou camst too soone, but now thou comst too late,
Thy force too great, but now it is too small,

Halfe had in Loue, but wholy now in hate,
Desired of some, but cursed now of all,
  Oft I confesse that I haue quakte before thee,
  But do thy worst, death now I care not for thee.

But dost thou thinke thou canst thy selfe excuse,
To say (alas) thou hast but done thine office,
Vnhappie hand whom so the heauens dost vse,
On such a Saint to execute thy seruice:
  But since it was the will of God to do it,
  His will be done, I can but yeeld vnto it.

Yet for the care that Vertue hath conceyued,
For losse of him that was his dearest loue,
And for the death that Honour hath receyued,
Where pacience doth the deadly passions proue,
  I cannot chuse although my hart would hide it,
  To shew my griefe so great I cannot bide it.

Oh that I had but so diuine a head.
As could bewray the sorrowes of my breast,
Or from the graue to raise againe the dead,
And not offend my God in my request:
  Or by a prayer I might the grace obtaine,
  To see the face of my desire againe.

But all in vaine, my wishes not auaile,
My wordes are winde and carrie none effect,
And with my griefe I feele my senses faile,
That Fortune thus should crosse me in affect:
  As by the losse of one sweet heauenly friend,
  My heart should die, and yet no dolor end.

End, no God wot, there is no end of griefe,
Where sad conceit will neuer out of minde,
And bootlesse hope to harpe vpon reliefe.
Where Care may seeke, and neuer Comfort find.

11

For in the world I had no ioy but one,
And all but death, nowe he is dead and gone.

Gone is my ioy, alas and well-away,
What shall I doo nowe all my loue is gone,
All my delight is falne vnto decay,
Onely but heauen I haue to hope vpon.
  Oh heauenly powers take pitie of my crie,
  Let me not liue, and see my Louer die,

Oh my loue, ah my loue, all my loue gone,
Out alas sillie wretch, well-away wo is me,
Of a friend, euer friend, such a friend none,
In the worlde, through the worlde, may the worlde see:
  Holy Saints, higher powers, heauens looke vpon me,
  Pitie me, comfort me, thus wo begone me.

My heauenly Loue, heauens lou'd as well as I,
Heauen was his care, and heauen was his content,
In heauen he liues, in heauen he cannot die,
From heauen he came, and to the heauens he went,
  Oh heauenly Loue, heauens will I looke for neuer,
  Till in the heauens I may beholde thee euer.

But what, me thinks I see a sudden chaunge,
The world dooth seeme to alter nature much,
The state of things is to my reason straunge,
And sorrowes such as there were neuer such.
  Such lacke of loue, such mourning for a friend,
  Such world of woes, as if the world should end.

Me thinkes I see the Queene of kinde affect,
Sighing and sobbing with such inward griefe,
As he that could consider the effect,
Might see a heart lie dead without reliefe:
  And in conceite so ouercome with care,
  It killes my heart to see her heauie fare.

Me thinkes I see a sight of armed horse,
Led in by boyes as if the men were dead,
Me thinkes I heare men murmure of a corse,
And gallant youthes go hanging of the head:
  Me thinkes I heare a thunder in the aire,
  Bids fare well Hope & looke vpon Dispaire.

Me thinkes I heare the trumpet drum and fife,
Sound all a mort, as if the world were done,
Me thinkes I see the'nd of vnhappie life,
Or second ioy since latter age begone.
  Me thinkes I heare the horror of the crie,
  As if the day were come that all should die.

Oh what I heare, oh what I feele and see,
Hold hart, helpe heauens, how can I longer liue,
But in the heauens there is no helpe for me,
Not all the world can any comfort giue:
  When death doth of my dearest friend depriue me.
  What can remaine in comfort to reuiue me.

Yet for the world shall witnesse what thou art,
Which in the world did leaue no like behinde:
I will set downe though short of thy desart,
The happie honour of thy heauenly minde,
  And on thy tombe I wil with teares engraue,
  The death of life that for thy lacke I haue.

Looke on the hils how all the Shepheards sit,
Heauie to thinke vpon their honest friend,
How Phillis sits as one besides her wit,
To see the sorrow of her Shepheards end:
  Harke how the Lambs go blaying vp & downe,
  To see their Shepheards caried to the towne.

Looke how the flock begin to leaue their feeding,
While cruell beasts breake in among the sheepe,

13

See how the heart of loue dooth lie a bleeding,
That Mars was slaine while Venus was a sleepe,
  See how the earth is bare in euerie place,
    To see that death hath done the worlde disgrace.

And Corridon poore sillie wretched swaine,
Dooth make such mone as if he should go mad,
All in dispaire to see good dayes againe,
To loose the ioy that on the earth he had:
  Who since the time he heard but of the wound,
    Liu'de like a ghost that goes vpon the ground.

And so forlorne abandonde all content,
Keepes in the Caues where comfort is vnknowne,
Borne but to liue, and onely to lament,
The dolefull life that by his death hath growne:
  Who in his life would let him know no care,
    But by his death all griefes that euer are.

Pan in a rage hath broken all his pipes,
Pallas alas sits poaring on a booke,
Her weeping eyes see howe Diana wipes,
And poore Apollo casts a piteous looke:
  The Nymphes come in with such a wofull crying,
    As if that Loue or Venus lay a dying.

The Nightingale is stopped in her throte,
And shriking Owles do make a fearefull noise,
The dolefull Rauens sing a deadly note,
And little Wrennes the end of Eagles ioyes:
  The Phoenix droopes, and Falcons beate their wings,
    To heare how Swans of death and sorrow sings.

The trees are blasted, and the leaues do wither,
The daintie greene is turnde to duskie gray,
The gallant Vines are shrunke and gone togither,
And all the flowers doo fade and fall away.

The springs are dried, and all the fish scale beaten,
And all good fruite the earth it selfe hath eaten.

Oh what a wo it is to see the woes,
Where nought but wo is left to looke vpon,
A griefe too great for Reason to disclose,
And in effect a death to studie on:
  Where man and beasts, birds, fishes, flowers and trees,
  Do halfe the hope of all their comfort leese.

When on the earth was euer such a sight,
Hardly the world can such a sorrow haue:
Neuer did death more seaze vpon delight,
Then when this knight was caried to his graue:
  Which when I sawe, so neere my heart I set,
  As while I liue I neuer can forget.

First comes the brother all in mourning blacke,
Mourning in deede in bodie and in minde,
Foulding his armes, as if his heart would cracke,
Feeling the death that Loue and Nature finde:
  Looking vpon the last of his delight,
  Oh heauenly God it was a pitious sight.

The Scholers come with Lachrimis Amoris,
As though their hearts were hopelesse of reliefe,
The Soldiers come with Tonitru Clamoris,
To make the heauens acquainted with their griefe:
  The noble Peeres in Ciuitatis portis,
  In hearts engrauen come with Dolor mortis.

The straungers come with Oh che male sorte,
The seruants come with Morte dila vita,
The secret friends with Morte púi che morte,
And all with these Felicita finita:
  Nowe for my selfe, Oh dolor infernale,
  Da videre morte, & non da viuere tale,

Now if the griefe of all the world be great,
How great is his that is the griefe of all,
Who doth in thoughts more deadly pangs repeate,
Then euer did to all the world befall,
  Whose paines and passions onely do approue,
  The onely true Anotamie of loue.

But since I see there is no remedie,
What God will haue, must neuer be withstoode:
And Male-content is but a maladie,
That may consume, but can doe little good,
  I will to God referre my whole reliefe,
  In heauenly care of my vnhappie griefe.

And on my knees beseech his holy will,
To cast on me those sweete and louing eyes,
That heale the heart of euery hatefull griefe,
And giue the life where comfort neuer dyes.
  And where my heart is gone, my hope may thether.
  That faith and loue may liue in heauen together.

But till my soule may see that heauenly sweete,
Where Vertue dooth her dearest loue embrace:
Where Comfort, Care and Kinde affect may meete,
And haue the ioy to see each others face:
  Vpon thy Tombe I will these wordes set downe,
  That all the world may read of thy renowne.
Finis.

(2)   *A pleasant Poem*

A Angels haue not their honour for their hue,
N No bewtie like the vertue of the minde,
N No life to loue that cannot proue vntrue,
E Esteeme the comfort of the highest kinde.

P Pure is the minde that cannot meane amisse,
A And sweete the life that is maintainde by loue,
R Rare is the heart where such affection is,
K Kinde the conceipt that dooth such honour proue,
E Excellens rare that wit and reason winneth,
R Read but each letter as the line beginneth.

                          Finis. A. P.

(3)   *Another*

T Time made a stay when highest powers wrought,
R Regard of loue where vertue had her grace,
E Excellence rare of euerie beautie sought,
N Notes of the heart where honour had her place,
T Tried by the touch of most approued truth,
A A worthie Saint to serue a heauenly Queene,
M More faire then she that was the fame of youth
E Except but one, the like was neuer seene.

                    Finis. Trentame.

(4)   *Another.*

G Good is the best, the most can say no more,
A And yet is good, and better, and the best,
R Reason requires the best be set before,
R Regard of loue findes reason in the rest,
E Except the best in euerie good excepted,
T Though better serue the good may be accepted.

                    Finis. Garet.

(5)　*A sweete Pastorall.*

Good Muse rocke me asleepe with some sweet harmonie,
　This weary eie is not to keepe, thy warie companie,
Sweet Loue be gone a while, thou knowst my heauines,
　Bewtie is borne but to beguile my heart of happines.
See how my litle flocke that lou'd to feed on hie,
　Do head-long tumble downe the rocke, & in the vally die.
The bushes and the trees, that weare so fresh and greene,
　Do all their daintie colours leese, and not a leafe is seene.
The Black-bird, & the Thrush, that made the woods to ring
　With all the rest are now at hush, & not a note they sing.
Sweet Philomele the bird, that hath the heauenly throte,
　Doth now (alas) not once afoord recording of a note.
The flowers haue had a frost, each hearbe hath lost her sauor,
　And Phillida the faire hath lost, the comfort of her fauor.
Now all these carefull sights, so kill me in conceit,
　That how to hope vpon delights, it is but meere deceit.
And therefore my sweet Muse, that knowst what help is best,
　Do now thy heauenly cunning vse to set my heart at rest.
And in a dreame bewray, what fate shall be my friend,
　Whether my life shall still decay, or when my sorow end.

(6)　*A Sonet.*

The prettie Turtle-doue, that with no little mone,
　When she hath lost her louing mate, sits mourning all alone,
The Swan that alwaies sings an houre before hir death,
　Whose deadly gripes do giue the grones, & draw away hir breath:
The Pellican that pecks the blood out of hir brest,
　And by her death doth only feed her yong ones in the nest,
The Hart imparked close with in a plot of ground,
　Who dare not ouer-looke the pale, for feare of hunters hound.
The Hound in kenell tied, that heares the chase go by,
　And bootles wishing foot abrode, in vaine doth howle & cry:
The Tree with withered top, that hath his branches dead,
　And hangeth down his hiest bowes, while other hold vp head:

Endure not halfe the death, the sorow nor disgrace,
  That my poore wretched mind abides, where none can wail my case.

For truth hath lost his trust, more deare then Turtle-doue,
  And what a death to such a life, that such a pain doth proue:
The Swan for sorrow sings to see her death so nie,
  I die because I see my death, and yet I cannot die:
The Pellican doth feed their young ones with their blood,
  I bleed to death, to feed desires that neuer do me good.
My heart imparked round within the ground of griefe,
  Is so beset with hounds of hate, it lookes for no reliefe.
And sweet desire my dogge, is clogged so with care,
  He cries and dies to heare delights, & come not where they are.
My tree of true delight, is sabd with sorrow so,
  As but the heauens do sooner helpe, will be his ouerthrow.
In summe, my dole, my death, and my disgrace is such,
  As neuer man that euer liu'd, knew euer halfe so much.

(7)   *A Poem.*

Go Muse vnto the Bower, whereas my mistres dwels,
  And tell her of her seruants loue, but tel her nothing els.
And speake but in her eare, that none may heare but she.
  That if she not the sooner helpe, there is no helpe for me.
Not that I feare to speake, but it is strange to heare,
  That shee will neuer looke on him, that holds her loue so deare.
Perhaps she knowes it not, or if she do she will not,
  Yet let her kindness haue a care, that though she hurt she kil not.
And though it be to strange, yet let her this beleue me,
  That dead men liue, yet I am dead, yet liue if she releue me,
For yet are not so colde the coales of kinde desire,
  But in the ashes liues a sparke, to kindle loue a fire,
Which fier his fuell hath, but from those fairest eies,
  Where faith doth burne & fancie flame, & fauor neuer dies.

(8)   *A Poem.*

Pure of the faire that neuer fadeth hue,
Exceeding sweet that euery sweet exceedeth:

Neere to the heauens where highest glaces growe'
Excellent fruit that such a fancie feedeth,
Loue in the eyes, and honour in the heart,
O Princes, Angelles Goddesse, heauenly feature,
Perfection farre aboue all natures arte,
Exception none, was euer such a creature.
Rich, vertuous, wise, faire, courteous, comely, kinde,
Ioy to the hearts of all that doo beholde her,
Courtly of grace, and of a princely minde,
High in the heauens, the Angels haue enrolde her.

(9)   *A Pastorall.*

Mine eyes haue seene the Idoll of my heart,
Mine eyes haue heard the wonder of the wise,
Mine heart hath toucht the comfort of mine eyes.

Nowe handes be true vnto your happie heart,
Tongue say thy heart shall all in silence serue,
Heart to thy head doo not thy thoughts impart,
Eyes see the sight that doth your sight preserue.

And nowe thou eye, thou tongue, thou hand and heart,
But looke, or speake, or touch, or turne awrie,
The heauens pronounce the due of your desart.
Be true and liue, but if a Traitor, die.

(10)   *A Poem.*

Like to an Hermit poore in place obscure.
I meane to spende my dayes in endlesse doubt:
To waile such woes as time cannot recure,
Where none but loue shall euer finde me out.
My foode shall be of care and sorrow made,
My drinke nought else but tears falne from mine eyes,
And for my light in such obscured shade,
The flames shall serue that from my heart arise.

A gowne of griefe my bodie shall attire,
And broken hope the staffe of all my stay,
Of late repentance linkt with long desire,
The Couch is made whereon my bones to lay,
And at my gate Dispaire shall linger still,
To let in Death when Loue and Fortune will.

(11)   *Of his Mistresse loue.*

To trie whose art and strength did most excell,
My Mistresse Loue and faire Diana met,
The Ladies three forthwith to shooting fell,
And for the prize the richest Iewell set.
Sweete Loue did both her bowe and arrowes gage,
Diana did her bewtie rare lay downe,
My Mistresse pawnde her crueltie and rage,
And she that wanne had all for her renowne:
It fell out thus when as the match was done,
My Mistresse gat the bewtie and the bowe,
And streight to trie the weapons she had wonne,
Vpon my heart she did a shaft bestow.
  By Bewtie bound, by Loue and Vigor slaine,
  The losse is mine where hers was all the gaine.

(12)   *Of a discontented minde.*

Poets come all, and each one take a penne,
Let all the heads that euer did invite,
Let Sorrow rise out of her darkest denne,
And helpe an heart an heauie tale to write.
And if all these or any one can touch,
The smallest part of my tormenting paine:
Then will I thinke my griefe is not so much,
But that in time it may be healde againe.
But if no one can once come neare the thought,
Of that I feele, and no man else can finde,
Then let him say that deare his cunning bought,
There is no death to discontented minde.

What ailes mine eies, or are my wits distraught,
Do I not see, or know not what I see,
No maruell though to see that wonder wrought,
That on the earth an other cannot be.
What ment the gods when first they did creat you,
To make a face to mocke all other features,
Angels in heauen will surely deadly hate you,
To leaue the world so full of foolish creatures.
Cheeks, that enchaine the highest harts in thrall,
Is it set downe such faire shall neuer fade you:
Hands, that the harts of highest thoughts appall,
Was not Minerua mad when she had made you,
Faire: looke on you, and fare well Bewties grace,
Wise: why your wits the wisest doth abash.
Sweet: where is sweet, but in your sweetest face,
Rich: to your will all treasure is but trash.
Oh how these hands, are catching at those eyes,
To feed this heart that onely liues vpon them,
Ah, of these hands what humors do arise,
To blind these eies that liue by looking on them.
But heart must faint that must be going from you,
And eies must weepe that in you lose their seeing,
Heauens be your place, where Angels better knowe you,
And earth is too base for such a Goddesse beeing.
Yet where you come among those hiest powers,
Craue pardon then for all these great offences,
That when you dwelt among those harts of ours
Your only eies did blind our wits and senses.
Now if you see my will aboue my wit,
Think of the good that all your graces yeeld you:
Amazed Muse must haue a madding fit,
Who is but mad that euer hath beheld you.

(14)   *A Sonet.*

Those eies that hold the hand of euery heart,
That hand that holds the heart of euery eye,

That wit that goes beyond all Natures art,
The sence too deepe for Wisedome to discrie.
  That eye, that hand, that wit, that heauenly sence,
  Doth shew my onely mistresse excellence.

Oh eyes that pearce into the purest heart,
Oh hands that hold the highest thoughts in trall,
Oh wit that weyes the depth of all desart,
Oh sence that shewe the secret sweete of all.
  The heauen of heauens with heauenly powers preserue thee.
  Loue but thy selfe, and giue me leaue to serue thee.

To serue, to liue, to looke vpon those eyes,
To looke, to liue, to kisse that heauenly hand,
To sound that wit that doth amaze the minde,
To know that sence, no sence can vnderstand.
  To vnderstand that all the world may know,
  Such wit, such sence, eyes, hands, there are no moe.

(15)   *A pastorall of Phillis and Coridon.*

On a hill there growes a flower,
  Faire befall the daintie sweete:
By that flower there is a bower,
  Where the heauenly Muses meete.

In that Bower there is a Chaire,
  Fringed all about with golde:
Where doth sit the fairest faire,
  That did euer eye beholde.

It is Phyllis faire and bright,
  She that is the shepheards ioy:
She that Venus did dispight,
  And did blind her little boy.

This is she the wise, the rich,
  And the world desires to see,

This is Ipsa quae the which,
  There is none but onely shee.

Who would not this fact admire,
  Who would not this Saint adore,
Who would not this sight desire,
  Though he thought to see no more.

Oh faire eyes yet let me see,
  One good looke, and I am gone,
Looke on me for I am hee,
  Thy poore sillie Corridon.

Thou that art the shepheards Queene,
  Looke vpon thy sillie Swaine:
By thy comfort haue been seene,
  Dead men brought to life againe.

(16)   *The complaint of a forsaken Louer.*

Let me go seeke some solitarie place,
In craggie rocks where comfort is vnknowne:
Where I may sit and waile my heauy case,
And make the heauens acquainted with my mone.

Where onely Eccho with her hollow voice,
May sound the sorrow of my hidden sence:
And cruell chance the crosse of sweetest choise,
Doth breed the paine of this experience.

In mourning thoughts let me my mind attire,
And clad my care in weedes of deadly wo:
And make Disgrace the graue of my desire,
Which tooke his death wherby his life did grow.
  And ere I die engraue vpon my tombe,
  Take heed of Loue, for this is louers doome.

(17)   *A prettie Fancie.*

Who takes a friend and trusts him not,
Who hopes of good and hath it not,

Who hath a Item and keepes it not,
Who keepes a Ioy and loues it not.
  The first wants wit, the second will,
  Carelesse the third, the fourth dooth ill.

(18)   *An Epitaph on the death of a noble Gentleman.*

Sorrow come sit thee downe, and sigh and sob thy fill,
  And let these bleeding bitter teares, be witnesse of thine ill.
See, see, how Vertue sits, what passions she doth proue,
  To thinke vpon the losse of him, that was her dearest loue.
Come Pallas carefull Queene, let all the Muses waite,
  About the graue, where buried is the grace of your conceite,
Poets lay downe your pennes, or if you needes will write,
  Confesse the onely day of loue hath lost her dawning light.
And you that know the Court and what beseemes the place,
  With griefe engraue vpon his tombe, he gaue al Courts a grace.
And you that keepe the fields, and know what valure is,
  Say all to soone was seene in this vntimely death of his.
Oh that he liu'd in earth, that could but halfe conceiue,
  The honour that his rarest heart was worthie to receive.
Whose wisdome farre aboue the rule of Natures reach,
  Whose workes are extant to the worlde, that all the world may teach.
Whose wit the wonder-stone, that did true wisdome tutch,
  And such a sounder of conceipt, as few or neuer sutch.
Whose vertues did exceede in Natures highest vaine,
  Whose life a lanthorne of the loue that surely liues againe.
Whose friendship faith so fast, as nothing could remoue him,
  Whose honourable courtesie made all the world to loue him.
What language but he spake: what rule but he had read:
  What thought so high: what sense so deep: but he had in his head.
A Phoenix of the world, whom fame doth thus commend,
  Vertue his life, Valor his loue, and Honor was his end.
Vpon whose tombe be writ, that may with teares be red,
  Here lies the flower of chiualrie that euer England bred.
Oh Heauens, vpon the earth was neuer such a day,
  That all conceits of all contents should all consume away.

25

Me thinkes I see a Queene come couered with a vaile,
  The Court all stricken in a dumpe, the Ladies weepe & waile.
The knights in carefull sighs bewaile their secret losse,
  And he that best conceales his griefe, bewrayes he hath a crosse.
Come scholers bring your bookes, let reason haue his right,
  Do reuerence vnto the corse, in honour of the knight.
Come Souldiers see the knight, that left his life so neere ye,
  Giue him a volley of your harts, that all the world may heare ye.
And ye that liue at home, and passe your time in peace,
  To helpe ye sing his doleful dirge, let sorrow neuer cease.
Oh could I mourne inough, that all the world may see,
  The griefe of loue for such a losse, as greater cannot bee.
Our Court hath lost a friend, our Countrey such a knight,
  As with the torment of the thought, hath turned day to night.
A man, so rare a man, did neuer England breed,
  So excellent in euery thing, that all men did exceed.
So full of all effects that wit and since may scan,
  As in his heart did want no part to make a perfect man.
Perfection farre aboue the rule of humaine sence,
  Whose heart was onely set on heauen, and had his honor thence.
Whose marke of hiest aime, was honour of the minde,
  Who both at once did worldly fame, and heauenly fauour finde.
Whome Vertue so did loue, and learning so adore,
  As commendation of a man, was neuer man had more.
Whom wise men did admire, whom good men did affect,
  Whom honest men did loue and serue, and all men did respect.
Whose care his Countries loue, whose loue his Countries care,
  Whose carefull loue considered wel, his country could not spare.
Oh Christ what ruthfull cries, about the world do ring,
  And to behold the heauie sighes it is a hellish thing.
The campe, the dolefull campe, comes home with all a Mort,
  To see the captaine of their care, come home in such a sort.
The Court, the solemne Court, is in a sudden trance,
  And what is he but is amazde to heare of his mischance,
The Citie shakes the head, as it had lost a piller,
  And kind affect is in such care, a little more would kill her,
Sweet Oxford sits and weepes, and Cambridge cries outright.

To loose the honour of their loue, and loue of their delight.
The Cleargie singing Psalmes, with teares beblot their booke,
  And all the schollers follow on with sad and heauy lookes.
The Muses and the Nymphes attired all in blacke.
  With tearing heares & wringing hands, as if their harts would cracke,
The father, wife, and friends, and seruants in degrees,
  With blubbred eies bewaile the life that faithfull loue did leese.
My selfe that lou'de him more, then he that knew him much,
  Will leaue the honour of his worth, for better wits to tutch.
And said but what I thinke, and that a number know,
  He was a Phoenix of a man I feare there are no mo.
To set him downe in praise with men of passed fame,
  Let this suffice who more deseru'de: I neuer read his name.
For this he was in right, in briefe to shew his praise,
  For Vertue, Learning, Valor, Wit, the honor of our dayes.
And so with honor ende, let all the world go seeke,
  So yong a man, so rare a man, the world hath not the like.
Whose onely corps consumes, whose Vertue neuer dies,
  Whose sweetest soule enioyes the sweet of highest Paradice.

(19)   *The summe of the former in foure lines.*

Grace, Vertue, Valor, Wit, Experience, Learning, Loue,
Art, Reason, Time, Conceite, Deuise, Discretion, Truth,
All these in one, and but one onely proue,
Sorrow in age, to see the end of youth.

(20)   *In the praise of his Mistresse.*

Poets lay downe your pennes, let fancie leaue to faine,
  Bid all the Muses go to bed, or get a better vaine.
Their Musicks are to base, to sound that sweet consaite,
  That on the wonder of the world, with wonder may awaite.
But if as yet vnknowne, there be some daintie Muse,
  That can do more then all the rest, and will her cunning vse.
Let her come whet her wits, to see what she can do,
  To that the best that euer wrote, come neuer neere vnto.
For Venus was a toy, and onely feigned fable,
  And Cressed but a Chawcers ieast, and Helen but a bable.

27

My tale shall be of truth, that neuer Treason taught,
  My Mistresse is the onely sweete, that euer Nature wrought.
Whose eyes are like those starres that keepe the hiest skies:
  Whose beautie like the burning Sunne, that blinds the clearest eies.
Whose haires are like those beames, that hang about the Sunne,
  When in the morning forth he steps, before his course be runne.
And let me touch those lips, by loue, by leaue, or lucke,
  When sweet affect, by sweet aspect, may yet some fauour sucke.
They are those little foldes, of Natures finest wit,
  That she sat smoothing while she wrought, & wilbe smacking yet.
And for that purest red, with that most perfect white,
  That makes those cheekes the sweetest chaines, of louers high delite.
What may be said but this. Behold the onely feature,
  That all the world that sees the face, may wonder at the creature.
I will not stand to muse as manie writers do,
  To seeke out Natures finest stuffe to like her lims vnto.
For if thou wert on earth that could in part compare:
  With euerie part of euerie part, wherein her prayses are.
Either for Natures gifts or Vertues sweetest grace:
  I would confesse a blinded heart, were in vnhappie case.
But where both Nature, Sense, and Reason doth approue,
  She is the onely Saint on earth, whom God and man doth loue.
Let this in summe suffice for my poore Muse and mee,
  She is the Goddesse of the earth and there is none but thee.

(21)   *Of Truth and Loue.*

Truth shewes her selfe in secret of her trust,
Wisedome her grace in honour of her Loue:
Vertue her life where loue is not vniust,
Loue in his sweete that dooth no sorrow proue.

Truth hath in hate to heare a fained tale,
Wisedome dooth frowne where follie is in place:
Honour is gone where Bewtie is too small,
And Vertue dyes where Loue is in disgrace.

I leaue your truth to your desired trust,
Your wisedome to the wonder of the wise:
Your highest ioy to iudgement of the iust,
Where Vertue liues, and Honour neuer dies.
  And he vouchsafe you that all truth preserueth,
  What Truth of Loue, and Loue of Truth deserueth.

(22)   *Rare newes.*

Newes from the heauens, all warres are at an end,
Twixt higher powers, a happie peace concluded,
Fortune and Faith are sworne each others friend,
And Loues desire shall neuer be deluded.

Time hath set downe the compasse of his course,
Nature her worke, and Excellence her art:
Care his content, and Crueltie his curse,
Labour his desire, and Honour his desart.

Wordes shall be deedes, and men shall be diuine,
Women all Saints or Angels in degrees:
Cloudes shall away, the Sunne shall euer shine,
Heauens shall haue power to hinder none of these.
  These are the Articles of the conclusion,
  Which when they fall, then looke for a confusion.

(23)   *Of a wearie life.*

Who can delight in such a wofull sound,
Or loues to heare a Laie of dire lament,
What note is sweete when griefe is all the ground,
Discords can yeeld but onely discontent.
  The wrest in wrung that straines each string too farre,
  And strifes the stops that giue each stroke a iarre.

Harsh is (alas) the harmonie God knowes,
When out of tune is almost euerie string:
That sound vnsweete that all of sorrow growes.
And sad the Muse that so is forst to sing.

But some doe sing but that for shame woulde crie,
So doth my Muse and so I sweare doe I.

Good Nature weepes to see her selfe abusde,
Ill Fortune shewes her furie in her face,
Poore Reason pines to see himselfe refusde,
And Dutie dies to see his sore disgrace.
  Hope hangs his head to see Dispaire so neere,
  And what but Death can end this heauie cheere.

But hold, each teare no token of a toy,
But torment such as teare my heart asunder,
Each sobbing sigh a signe of such annoy,
As how I liue, beleeue me t'is a wonder.
  Each grone a gripe that makes me gaspe for breath,
  And euery straine a bitter pangue of death.

Loe thus I liue, but looking still to die,
And still I looke, but still I see in vaine,
And still in vaine, alas, I lie and crie,
And still I crie, but haue no ease of paine.
  So still in paine I liue, looke, lie and crie,
  When Hope will helpe, or Death will let me die.

(24)   *Of his vnhappie state of life.*

If euer man did liue in Fortunes scorne,
Whose ioyes do faile that feele distresse in minde:
Whose yeres with cares, whose eies with teares beswolne
That in each part, all parts of griefes doth find.
  To grace his ill, send such a man to me,
  That am more haplesse then himselfe can be.

For good desart that is vnkindly vsed,
For seruice, loue and faith that findeth hate:
Who in his Mistresse eyes is most refused,
Whose comforts faile, whose succours come too late,
  If that man liue that in his life findes this,
  Know hee my chance, for my hap harder is.

30

If damning bowes be but as dreames regarded,
And constant thoughts as shewes of custome taken:
If any man for loue be thus rewarded,
And hath his hopes for these vnrights forsaken.
  Let him see me whose like hath neuer beene,
  Kilde by these wrongs, and yet by death vnseene.

Then by this riuall of my such dispise,
With much desire shall seeke my name to know:
Tell him my lines Strange things may well suffice,
For him to beare, for me to seeke them so.
  And t'was inough that I did finde such euils,
  And t'were too much that Angels should be diuels.

(25)   *His complaint against Loue and Fortune.*

If Heauen and earth were both not fullie bent,
To plague a wretch with an infernall paine:
To robbe the heart of all his high content,
And leaue a wound that should not heale againe.
If cruell Fortune did not seeke to kill,
The carefull spirit of my kinde affect:
And care did not so crucifie me still,
That Loue had left no hope of his effect.
If she whom most my heart hath euer loued,
Were not vnkinde in care of my distresse:
And she by whom my griefe might be remoued,
Did not holde backe the meane of my redresse.
If all these thoughts and many thousands mo,
Too long to tell, too deadly to endure:
Did not consume my heart in sorrow so,
That care hath left no hope of any cure.
Then might I yet amid my greatest griefe,
Perswade my pacience with some heauenly power,
That when I most despaire of my reliefe,
My hopelesse heart might find some happie bower.
But since that Fortune so doth frowne vpon me,
That care hath thus of comfort all bereft me:

31

Thinke it not strange to see me wo begone me,
Where no good hope of no good hap is left me.
And since I see all kindness so vnkinde,
And friendship growne to such contrarie thought:
And such a thought the torment of the minde,
That care and sorrow hath consumed to nought.
I will resolue (though pacience be perforce)
To sit me downe, and thus in secret crie:
Dead is my heart, oh earth receiue my corse,
Heauen be my life, for in the world I die.

(26)   *In the praise of his Penelope.*

When authors write god knowes what thing is true,
Did Homer wrote of fine Vlysses wit,
And Ouid wrote of Venus heauenly hue.
And Ariosto of Orlandos fit.
  One wrote his pleasure of Caliope,
  I am to write of sweete Penelope.

And where each one did shewe a secret vaine,
And whether that Vlysses were or not,
And though that Ouid did but onely faine,
And Ariosto set downe many a blot.
  And some wrote loudly of Caliope,
  I write but truth of sweete Penelope.

And if I had Vlysses skilfull sconce,
With Homers pen and Ouids heauenly voice,
I would set downe a wonder for the nonce,
To set them all a newe to worke againe.
  And he that wrote of his Caliope.
  Should hush to heare of this Penelope.

As true as she that was Vlysses wife,
As faire as she whom some a Goddesse faine,
A Saint of shape, and of more vertuous life,
Then she for whom Orlandos knight was slaine.

In euerie thing aboue Caliope,
There is none such as sweete Penelope.

And for this time go looke the world that will
For constant faire, for vertue and good grace,
For euery part in whom no part is ill,
For perfect shape, and for a heauenly face,
  Angellica, Venus, Caliope,
  All are but blows vnto Penelope.

(27)   *A Poem.*

Looke not too long vpon those lookes, & blinds the ouerlooker sore,
& if you speak, speak not to much, least speaking once & speak no more:
Think not but what it is to think, to reach beyond the reach of thought,
And if you do, do what you can, when you haue don you can do nought,
But if you see against your will, looke but away and be not slaine,
And if a worde go vnawares, with care it may be calde againe.
And for a thought it is not hurt, except it grow vnto a thing,
But to vndo that hath bene done, is onely conquest of a king.
But since in thee O silly wretch, both sight, & speach, & thought and deed.
By reason of a wrong conceit, do but thine owne confusion breed.
Shut vp thy eies, seale vp thy tongue, lock vp thy thought, lay downe thy head
And let thy mistres see by this, how loue hath struck her seruant dead.
And that but in her heauenly eye, her worde, her thought, and onely will
Doth rest the dead, to kill the quite, or else to cure thee of this ill.

(28)   *A Poem.*

Powre downe poore eies the teares of true distresse,
Heare but (oh heauens) the horror of my crie,
Iudge of the care that can haue no redresse,
Let me not liue to see my louer die.
  In sorrowes rules, like sorrow neuer read,
  Phillip sweet-knight, sweet Phillip Sidney dead.

Paine more then art, or Nature can expresse,
Hell to the world to loose a heauenly friend,
Ioy is become but sorrow and distresse,

Life with my Loue let death and dolor end.
  In bitter teares hath hart of honor blead,
  Past hope of helpe to see perfection dead.

(29)   *A Poem.*

Peace all the world, your weeping is but vaine,
Heauen hath the hope of honor all away:
Ioy but in heauen to meet that hope againe,
Lincke with the life that neuer can decay.
  In this alone all hope of comfort lies.
  Perfection onely liues in Paradice.

(30)   *A Poem.*

Perfection peereles, Vertue without pride,
Honor and learning linckt with highest Loue,
Ioy of the thought in true discretion tride,
Loue of the life that highest honors proue.
  In Angels armes with heauenly hands embraced,
  Paradice pleased, and all the world disgraced.

Seeke all the world, oh seeke and neuer finde,
In earthly mould the mount of such a minde:
Diuinest gifts that God on man bestoweth,
No glory such as of such glory groweth.
  End of the ioyes that hath all griefe begun,
  Yet let me weepe when all the world is done.

(31)   *Vpon a scoffing laughter giuen by a Gentlewoman*

Laugh not too much, perhaps you are deceyued,
All are not fooles that haue but simple faces:
Mists are abroad, things may be misconceyued,
Frumps and disdaines are fauours in disgraces.
  Now if you do not know what meane these speeches,
  Fooles haue long cotes, and Monkies haue no breeches.

Tihee againe, why what a grace is this,

34

Laugh a man out before he can get in:
Fortune so crosse, and fauour so amis,
Doomsday at hand before the world begin.
  Marie sir then but if the weather holde,
  Bewtie may laugh, and Loue may be a colde.

Yet leaue betimes your laughing tootoo mutch,
Or find the Foxe, and then begin the chase:
Shut not a Rat within a sugar hutch,
And thinke you haue a Squirrell in the place.
  But when you laugh let this go for a iest,
  Seeke not a Woodcocke in a Swallowes nest.

(32)   *A sweete contention between Loue,*
          his Mistresse, and Bewtie.

Loue & my Mistres were at strife who had the greater power on me,
  Betwixt them both oh what a life, nay what a death is this to be.
She said she did it with her eie: he said he did it with his dart,
  Betwixt them both (a sillie wretch) t'is I that haue the wounded hart.
She said she only spake the word, that did enchant my pearing sence,
  He said, he onely gaue the sound, that entred hart without defence,
She said they were her onely heares, on which the daintie Muses waite:
  He said he was the onely meane, that entred Muses in conceite.
She said her Bewtie was the marke, that did amaze the highest mind:
  He said he onely made the mist, whereby the sences grew so blind.
She said, that onely for her sake, the best would venture life and lim:
  He said she was too much deceiu'd, they honoured her because of him.
Long while (alas) she would not yeeld, but it was she that rul'de the rost,
  Vntill by proofe she did confesse, if he were gone her ioy was lost.
And then she cried, oh daintie Loue, I now do find it is for thee,
  That I am lou'd and honored both, & thou hast power to conquer me,
But when I heard her yeeld to Loue, oh how my hart did leape for ioy,
  That now I had some little hope, to haue an end of mine annoy.
For though that Fancie Bewtie found, a power all to pitilesse,
  Yet Loue would neuer haue the hart, to leaue his seruant comfortles:
But as too soone before the field, the trumpet sounds the ouerthrow,
  So all too soone I ioyed too much, for I awaked and nothing so.

Come solemne Muse and helpe me sing,
  A dolefull note, a dying song,
What wretched cares my heart do wring,
  To see howe death hath done me wrong.

For I haue lost (oh deadly wo)
  My iem, my ioy, my life, my loue,
And in the world their is no mo,
  Can heale the paine that I do proue.

My sweete affections all are fled,
  Desires, delights, and all are gone,
My heart is sicke, my hope is dead,
  And onely death to looke vpon.

These secrete cares so kill my heart,
  With inward gripes of endlesse griefe,
That how can sorrow euer pare.
  Where is no hope to haue reliefe.

But helpelesse still I lie.
  consuming so in secret care:
That who doth liue and would not die,
  To looke vpon my heauie face.

But all in vaine I make this mone,
  Where nothing can my griefe release,
For I am onely left alone,
  To sorrow still and neuer cease.

But sorrow now euen do thy wurst,
  For death in fine will be a friend:
For I do know my heart will burst,
  And then thy force will haue an end.

36

Faire, is to base for Natures excellence,
Rich, all too meane for such a mind of treasure:
All, but too few to do her reuerence,
Vertue her selfe doth loue her out of measure.
No earthly coast containeth such a creature,
Chose by heauens, to shew the earth a wonder:
Ioy of the earth, the miracle of Nature,
Sent to the wise to set all wits asunder,
How farre she is aboue all humane sence,
Aske of the Gods for men cannot discerne:
When such I find her secret excellence,
As wit and reason are too weake to learne.
  Rare is the worke that Nature thus hath ended.
  Daintie the end that cannot be amended.

(35)   *Diana virgin, her complaint to the Goddesse Diana.*

Oh sweet Diana that dwelst among the nimphs,
In whom the fire of Nature hath no force:
Whose heauenly eye beholds those silly imps,
Whose ruthfull harts do sue for thy remorce.
Vouchsafe, oh saint, from that pure hand of thine,
Some pities helpe, to this poore hart of mine.

Was it my fault that Cupid found the meane,
First to creepe in, into thy quiet Court,
My hope was cleare, my comfort had bene cleane,
From any hap of such vnhappie hurt:
  But well I see amid the greatest cares,
  A sudden heart may slippe in vnawares.

Alas, alas, full little did I thinke,
The little thing had had so great a power:
I thought him blind when he did onely winke,
And sweet his thoughts, that fall out deadly sower.

But since I was thus trapped in this traine,
Once set my heart at libertie againe.

But Ladie say, is Loue of such a force,
That onely death must heale the desperate wound:
In heauenly thoughts hath Reason no remorce.
In cure of loue was neuer comfort found.
  Hath Cupid force to come and coniure thee,
  Oh no, alas, it is to conquer mee.

T'was I, t'was I that onely had the hap,
To take the hurt the wretched Traitor wrought:
T'was onely I, that caught the secret clap,
While carefull faith with cruell fancie fought.
  T'was I Diana, and t'is onely I,
  Whom thou must helpe, or els I yeeld to die.

(36)   *Brittons vision of Cupids complaint against his*
        fowle father Vulcan for begetting him.

Within the thicke of most vnquiet thoughts,
Where Wit and Will had long each other lost:
With carefull sence of sweete desire I sought,
Which was the way that Fancie followed most:
  And passing on the path that they did proue,
  Plodding along I met with pitious Loue.

Wholy disarmde, and hanging downe the head,
Blinded: oh no, but all with blubbred eyes:
Falne in the face with colour pale and dead,
Wringing his hands in such a wofull wise.
  That when I saw how he had wept and cried,
  Truely I thought the wretch would there haue died.

But when I sawe the little thing alone,
Farre from himselfe thus wander too and fro:
And when I heard howe he did still bemone,
Some hidden cause that I desirde to know.

Close in conceite, I hid my selfe, to heare,
What was the cause of this his heauie cheare.

Thus as I sat close hidden from his sight,
Of Lucklesse Loue lamenting of his losse:
This sillie wretch in this most sorrowed plight,
With sighes and sobs, and grieuous grones God wote,
　Cursing and banning Bewties generation,
　Thus did begin his wofull lamentation.

Oh haplesse hower when first my mother made,
The cursed match with that vncomely Smith:
Whose smokie forge hath made her beautie fade,
As farre vnfit for her to meddle with.
　Whose filthie face doth set foorth such a feature,
　As hell it selfe hath scarce so fowle a creature.

But what conceite her frantike fancie fead,
To match with him that was so fowle a match:
Alas, alas, was Mercurie so dead,
So great a prince to looke on such a patch.
　Needes must she thinke as she did after proue,
　Vulcan was not a man for Venus loue.

Oh smokie fowle ill fauoured filthie theefe,
Howe could thy mind so high a matter moue:
Howe could thy heart haue hope to find releese,
Looke on thy selfe, and neuer looke for loue.
　So faire, so fowle, such contraries agree,
　Reason would sweare that it should neuer bee.

Better I were to be a bastard borne,
Then haue a father of so fowle a hue:
Rather I wish that thou shouldst weare the horne,
Then that the world should thinke it to be true.
　That Cupid sweete should haue so fowle a Sire,
　And hath his face still soyled in the fire.

See wretched dogge the summe of thy disgrace,
First thou hast wrought my mother great defame:
Next thou hast set a marke vpon thy face,
That all the world doth laugh to heare thy name:
  And last for me they say how can it bee,
  That he was sonne to such a slaue as hee.

But fie vpon that filthie face of thine,
Those mouldie chaps to touch my mothers face:
I do protest my conscience doth repine,
That you shouldst kisse her in another place
  But ugly beast into some hole go hide thee,
  For Bewtie sweares that Loue can not abide thee.

Oh Mars, oh Mars, where are those stately strokes,
That left the field so ouer-flowen with blood:
That cloue downe hils, and threw downe sturdie Okes,
And made the aire come thundring through the wood:
  Art thou so weake with bending of one blade,
  Thou canst not breake the chaine that Vulcan made.

Vp man, arise and shew thy manly strength,
Least that the Smith do seeke my mothers shame:
Lie not too long least slugguish slouth at length,
Seeke by desart the honour of thy name:
  Vulcan is gone, but Cupid hath a file,
  To loose the locke that may the Smith beguile.

But come away, for looke where Vulcan comes,
But thou art loose now let him do his woorst:
Looke how the theefe comes biting of his thumbs,
Cursing the happe that hath his cunning burst.
  But let him fome and bristle like a bore,
  Let him be sure to catch thee so no more.

But mother fie, what fond affect was that,
To looke on Vulcan in the vaine of loue;

Confesse a truth, you did you knew not what,
When pacience would so vile a matter proue.
  Was want of sight that wrought your ouerthrow.
  Why then (alas should I be blinded so.

But mother, no: there is an other thing,
Who is so blind as they that will not see:
A base conceite sometime may stoope a king,
I see in some that see not into mee.
  Better it is with Bewtie to be blinded,
  Then Bewties grace to be blindly minded.

But will you know it was no worke of mine,
Follies effect committed all the fact:
Although your words haue made poore Cupid whine,
To say that I was authour of the act:
  But will or nill I must my selfe content,
  For parents faults poore children must be shent.

I am the child I cannot but confesse,
The world doth say that I am Venus sonne:
By whom begot I heare of nothing lesse,
But might I heare by whom the deed was donne:
  In such desire as might the world defie,
  There could not liue a gladder man then I.

Once Vulcans sonne I know I cannot be,
Mars was the man came neerer to the marke:
As for the Smith it neuer could be hee,
A Bunting neuer could beget a Larke,
  Oh no, the world is much deceiu'd in mee.
  I hope to finde an other pedegree.

I am the sonne of secret sweet conceite,
Got by Desire and bred vp by desart:
Nurst by the mind that neuer meant deceite,
Fed with the fauour of a faithfull heart.

High from the heauens I tooke my happy name,
Where Venue liues, and Vulcan neuer came.

Begot I was in Anno out of minde,
Borne in a countrie that no creature knowes:
Bred in a world that worldings cannot finde,
Fed with a fruit that in no garden growes.
  Lodge in an eye that neuer can destroy me,
  Kept in a hart that neuer can come nigh me.

Loe thus I liue where I can neuer die,
Fearing no hap, nor looking after hope:
Pleasing my selfe with pleasures farre and nie,
Wanting no wish where will hath such a scope:
  Gouerning all, where none can gouerne me,
  Oh what a king may daintie Cupid be.

Then leaue to mourne, and let the world perceiue,
That Poets fancies are but fained fables,
And Ouid did but studie to deceiue,
Such kind conceites as loue such foolish bables.
  For he that lookes into Mineruas ioy,
  Shall say that Cupid is a daintie boy.

What that me thought the little wagge arose,
And gathered colour pretily in his face:
And standes me op a tip-toe on his toes,
Vaunting himselfe with such a Venus grace:
  As droue my heart into so great a laughter,
  That I awooke, and neuer saw him after.

(37)   *Brittons second dreame of Venus complaint*
        when she lost her son Cupid.

But sorrow thus to lose the sight of loue,
Scarce well awakt I fell asleepe againe:
In hope the heauens would some odde humor moue,
To shew the fruits of such a sleepie vaine:

42

And scarce a sleepe strange visions did ensue,
  Yet not so strange but that they may be true.

Hard by the place where I had Cupid seene,
Me thought I saw a heauenly kind of creature,
Of stature tall, of countenance like a Queene,
Exceeding faire, and of so sweet a feature:
  That when I stood to view her stately grace,
  My thought indeed I saw an Angels face.

Attirde she was in garments white as snow,
Saue on her arme she wore a Tawnie lace,
In her right hand she barę a bended bowe,
And at her backe an emptie Arrow case:
  Little she said that I could heare at first,
  But sight and sobt as if her hart would burst.

But yet at last with sad and heauie looke,
She tooke the bow and flung it on the ground:
And from hir backe the emptie case she tooke,
Which with the lace vnto the bowe she bound,
  Then downe she sate within a shadow vaile,
  And to her selfe she tolde this heauie tale.

Was euer wretch or creature thus beguilde,
To loose the iewell of his chiefest ioy:
Can Venus choose but sorrow for her childe.
No, no, my darling was a daintie boy:
  But Mars, oh Mars, what ment he to come hither,
  For Mars and he are gone away together.

These little things were wont to be his armes,
But now the wag hath throwne these toyes away:
And thinks himselfe amid the thickest harmes,
In onely hope to finde a happie day:
  Oh hawtie reach of honors high renowne,
  That throwes the sence of sweetest humors downe,

But my sweet boy, when first these hands did binde thee,
I knew each way that thou wert woont to go,
And when this heart (vnhappie did vnbind thee,
I little thought thou shouldst haue rannged so.
  But come againe good wretch let me intreat thee.
  And I protest thy mother will not beat thee.

But turne againe and tell me ere thou goest,
Doest thou intend to do som royall thing:
Let this suffice that I am sure thou knowest,
My hart could wish that thou wert made a king.
  God send thy hart the height of thy desier,
  Hope, hap & heauen, and who can wish thee hier.

And therewithall she bid those teares let fall,
That shewd the war where Loue & Reason fought,
Whose colour pale shewed somewhat did apall,
Her pacient heart with some vnhappie thought.
  And so sweet Saint with sorrow ouercome,
  She stood amazde as she were striken dombe.

Then I behelde a sight of daintie Nymphes,
Did straight before her stately eyes appeare:
And downe on knees fell all these heauenly impes,
To comfort her amid her heauie cheare.
  And when she heard that euery one had spoken,
  Peace, peace quoth she, for Bewties hart is broken.

Alas, Alas, ye little sillie things,
God knowes, I know still little do you know,
What do belong vnto the state of Kings,
What sets them vp, or seekes their ouerthrow.
  What kind of care do breed their sorrow most,
  What death is life wher dearest friends are lost.

But wish I yet I had but such a friend,
As by desert delight did holde full deare:

And feare by force did see his fatall end,
Yet no conceit could serue to keepe him heare.
  Would it not grieue each vaine within her hart,
  To see so sweet and deare a friend depart.

Then let this be a sparke of all my paine,
Alas, alas, t'is but a sparke in deed:
My sorrow sinks into so deepe a vaine,
As makes the hart of highest fauour bleed,
  The chiefest staffe of my assured stay,
  With no small griefe is gone, is gone away.

My Cupid was to me a child of loue,
But no such babe as ioied in childrens bables:
For mark his life, his mind would soone approue,
Such feined fancies were but Ouids fables.
  Who was as far from knowing my Cupido,
  As faithfull loue is farre from foule Libido.

He neuer liued by deedes of vaine desire,
Nor wrapt himselfe in Carpets of conceite:
But hautie Fame had set his heart on fire,
To shew the mind that neuer ment deceite.
  But seekes by armes to pul ambition downe,
  That wrought by force to wring me from my crowne.

O care most rare, and worthy kinde regarde,
O rare regard, and worthie high renowne:
O high renowne that rightly maist reward,
The carefull heart to keepe me in my crowne.
  And honor seekes where due desert may beare it,
  Which wonne by force, with fauor he shall weare it.

Wherewith (me thought) I heard a sudden larme,
To horse, to horse the Caualiroes cried,
And after that a crie of arme, arme, arme,
And downe they ranne vnto a riuer side.

Where I might heare the trumpet, drumme, and fife,
Sound vp the honour of a souldiers life.

Anon I saw the shippes drawe nigh the shore,
And all aboord went horse and man apace:
Where launching out the gunnes shot off so sore,
As where I stood did seemt to shake the place.
  And Trumpets shrill so sounded in the streame,
  As I awooke, and all was but a dreame.

(38)   *A deuice of Diogenes Tubbe.*

Diogenes was tearmed but a Dogge,
Tide to a Tubbe where lay but little treasure:
Who for his life was counted but a Hogge,
That knewe no part of any worldly pleasure.
  What said the king yet in his greatest throne,
  Either himselfe Dogenes, or none.

For when the king did bid him aske and haue,
His minde was not of any masse of wealth:
He askt no more then other creatures haue,
The chiefest comfort of his happie health.
  Take not away (quoth he) thou canst not giue,
  Out of the Sunne, for by the same I liue.

The good poore soule doth thinke no creature harme,
Onely he liues obscurely in his Tunne,
Most is his care to keepe his carkas warme,
All his delight to looke vpon the Sunne:
  And could the heauens but make the Sunne to know him
  He should not liue should keepe his shining fro him.

(39)   *A Metaphor.*

A little fire doth make the faggot burne,
When blowing much will put the fire out:
Silence but seld doth serue the louers turne,
And too much sute, for fauour hath a floute.

Then let thus much suffice for my desire,
The smallest blowing make the greatest fire.

Conceite is quicke, would so were sweete content,
Eyes hath a glaunce of too too great a grace:
Spirits do speake in silence of intent,
And thoughts are spirites of a secret place.
  In silence then let heart in sunder breake,
  Eyes shall behold, but spirites shall not speake.

(40)   *Of the birth and bringing vp of desire.*

When wert thou born Desire: in pompe and prime of Day:
By whom sweet boy wert thou begot: by good conceit men say
Tell me who was thy nurse: Fresh youth in sugred ioy:
What was thy meat and dayly food: sore sighes with great annoy.
What had you then to drinke: vnfained louers teares:
What cradle were you rocked in: in hope deuoide of feares.
What brought you then a sleepe: sweet speach that liked men best:
And where is now your dwelling place: in gentle hearts I rest.
Doth companie displease: it doth in many one:
Where would Desire then choose to be: he likes to muse alone.
What feedeth most your sight: to gaze on fauour still:
Who find you most to be your foe: Disdaine of my good will.
Will euer age or death bring you vnto decay:
No, No, Desire both liues and dies ten thousand times a day.

                                        Finis. E. of Ox.

(41)   *A pleasant Sonet.*

I will forget that ere I sawe thy face,
I will forget thou art so braue a wight:
I will forget thy stately comely grace,
I will forget thy hue that is so bright:
  I will forget thou art the fairest of all,
  I will forget thou winnest the golden ball.

I will forget thy forehead featly framde,
I will forget thy Christall eyes so cleere:
I will forget that no part may be blamde,
I will forget that thou hadst nere thy peere.

47

I will forget Vermelion is thy hue,
I will forget there is no Saint but thou.

I will forget thy dimpled chin so fine.
I will forget to approch thy seemely sight:
I will forget throughout the world so wide,
I will forget nones bewtie halfe so bright:
  I will forget thou stainst the brightest starre,
  I will forget thou passest Cynthea farre.

I will forget that feature is thy pheere,
I will forget thy bewtie dims the Sunne:
I will forget that hue not comes thee neere,
I will forget thy fame will nere be donne.
  I will forget thou art the fairest of all,
  That euer was, or is, or euer shall.
      And then
I will forget when grew my withered stalke,
I will forget to eate, to drinke, or sleepe:
I will forget to see, to speake, to walke,
I will forget to mourne, to laugh, to weepe.
  I will forget to heare, to feele, or taste,
  I will forget my life and all at last.
      And now
I will forget the place where thou dost dwell,
I will forget thy selfe, and so fare well.

(42)   *Another sweete Sonet.*

I seeke the thing that I do dayly see,
And faine would gaine that is already wonne,
I follow that which doth not from me flee:
Nor neuer seekes my companie to shunne.
  I granted am what I do seeme to craue,
  Yet lo I want, that fainest I would haue.

Hard is my hap since I am forst to ioy.
Where as there doth no ioy at all remaine:

And seeke for blisse where rests nought but annoy,
And for good will reape nought but deepe disdaine:
  Lucklesse my lot I labour but in vaine,
  I seeke to winne what I see others gaine.

Seeing hope, and hap, and all at once doth faile,
And that despaire is nowe my chiefest guide:
Whereby I see no ransome will me baile,
Out of the bondes wherein I now am tide,
  I am content in bondage for to serue,
  Vntill my faith my freedome doe deserue.

(43)   *A Poem.*

H Honour of loue, when loue in honour is,
O Olde men admire, and yong men are amazed:
P Perfection rare where nothing is amisse,
T The glasse of grace where eyes are ouer-gazed:
O Onely the face of such a heauenly feature,
N Not on the earth can be a fairer creature.

(44)   *A Sonet.*

Eye lie awake in hope of blessed seeing,
Hope thought that happe was ouer-long in lingring:
In came the Lasse, oh my thrise happie beeing,
Sences thought long vntil they were a lingring.

Tongue spar'd to speake, least it should speake too sparing,
Hart drownd in feare rauisht, denied her honour:
Handes sawe the price and long to be a sharing,
Pittie said, holde, but Courage cried, vpon her.

Silent she stood, yet in her silent speaking,
Wordes of more force then is great loue his thunder:
Ioyes weare her eyes, sorrowes asunder breaking,
Sweete was her face, each member was a wonder.

Heauen is hers, to her by heauens assigned,

49

Skies are her thoughts where pleasant Planets raigned,
Franke is her minde, to no ill craft inclined,
Loue is the crosse wherein her heart is chained.

Blisse was to see her steps to bedward bending,
Musicke to heare her selfe, herselfe vnlacing,
Straunge the aspect of two sonnes then discending,
Sweete was the kisse, but sweeter the imbracing.

(45)   *Another fine Sonet.*

Who deales with fire may burne his fingers ends,
And water drownes the foote that goes too deepe:
A lauish tongue will quickly loose his friends.
And he a foole that can no counsell keepe.
  Yet where desire doth egge the tongue to speake,
  Somewhat must out, or else the heart will breake.

To speake but truth deserue no deadly blame,
Though truth mistane sometime be pettie treason:
Yet causelesse death deserueth no defame,
Though ruthlesse rage will neuer yeeld to reason:
  Then since desire doth egge me on so sore,
  Truth will I speake although I speake no more.

The truth is this, there is no fire to loue,
Nor water like to Bewties heauenly brookes,
No friend to faith, to talke for hearts behoue,
Nor wit so wise to liue by onely lookes:
  Nor sweet desire by silence entertained,
  Nor kind Aspect, that euer loue disdained.

(46)   *A Pastorall.*

Sweet birds that sit and sing amid the shadie vallies,
And see how sweetly Phillis walks amid her garden allies:
Go round about her bower and sing, as ye are bidden,
To her is only knowne his faith, that from the world is hidden.
And she among you all that hath the sweetest voice,
To chirpe of him that neuer told, yet neuer changd his choise.

And not forget his faith, that liu'd for euer lou'd,
Yet neuer made his fancie knowne, nor euer fauour mou'd,
And euer let your ground of all your grace be this,
To you, to you, to you the due of loue and honour is,
On you, on you, on you, our musicke all attendeth,
For as on you our Muse begun, in you all musicke endeth.

(47)   *Coridons supplication to Phillis.*

Sweet Phillis if a sillie Swaine,
  may sue to thee for grace:
See not thy louing shepheard slaine,
  With looking on thy face.
But thinke what power thou hast got,
  Vpon my flocke and mee:
Thou seest they now regard me not,
  But all doe follow thee.

And if I haue so farre presuued,
  With prying in thine eyes:
Yet let not comfort be consumed,
  That in thy pitie lyes.
But as thou art that Phillis faire,
  That Fortune fauour giues,
So let not loue die in dispaire,
  That in thy fauour liues.

The Deere do bruise vpon the brier,
  The birds do pricke the cheries,
And will not Bewtie grunnt Desire,
  One handfull of her berries.
If so it be that thou hast sworne,
  That none shall looke on thee:
Yet let me know thou dost not scorne,
  To cast a looke on mee.

But if thy Bewtie make thee prowde,
  Thinke then what is ordained:

The heauens haue neuer yet allowed,
  That Loue should be disdained.
Then least the Fates that fauour Loue,
  Should curse thee for vnkinde.
Let me report for thy behoue,
  The honour of thy minde.

Let Coridon with full consent,
  Set downe what he hath seene:
That Phillida with Loues content,
  Is sworne the Shepheards Queene.

(48)   *A Sonet.*

Her face, her tongue, her wit,
  So faire, so sweete, so sharpe:
First bent, then drew, then hit,
  Mine eye, mine eare, mine hart.

Mine eye, mine eare, mine heart,
  To like, to learne, to loue:
Your face, your tongue, your wit,
  Doth lead, doth teach, doth moue.

Her face, her tongue her wit,
  With beame, with sound, with art:
Doth binde, doth charme, doth rule,
  Mine eye, mine eare, mine heart.

Mine eye, mine eare, mine heart,
  With life, with hope with skill,
Your face, your tongue, your wit.
  Doth feed, doth feast, doth fill.

Oh face, oh tongue, oh wit,
  With frownes, with checks, with smart:
Wring not, vex not, moue not,
  Mine eye, mine eare, mine hart.

This eye, this eare, this heart,
  Shall ioy, shall bind, shall sweare:
Your face, your tongue, your wit,
  To serue, to loue, to feare.

(49)   *A Louers complaint.*

Who knowes his cause of griefe,
  And can the same descrie:
And yet finds no reliefe,
  Poore wretch but onely I.

What foule will seeke the snare,
  That he be caught thereby:
If thereof he be ware,
  Poore wretch but onely I.

What fish will bite the baite,
  If he the hooke espie:
Or if he see deceite,
  Poore wretch but onely I,

Who's hee will seeke to mount,
  The toppe of Turrets hie,
To fall that makes account,
  Poore wretch but onely I.

Who's hee will scale the height,
  Of AEtna hill to frie:
So deare to bie-delight,
  Poore wretch but onely I.

The Hart will shunne the toyle,
  If he perceiue it lie:
No one would take such foyle,
  Poore wretch but onely I.

Who seekes to get and gaine,

The things that fates denie:
Must liue and die in paine,
  Poore wretch as now do I.

And heare my plaints to finish,
  In Lymbo lake I lie:
My griefe you must diminish,
  Poore wretch, or else I die.

(50)   *A Shepheards dreame.*

A Sillie Shepheard lately sate,
  among a flocke of sheepe:
Where musing long on this and that,
  At last he fell a sleepe.

And in the slumber as he lay,
  He gaue a piteous grone:
He thought his sheepe were runne away,
  And he was left alone.

He whopt, he wistled, and he calde,
  But not a sheepe came neere him:
Which made the shepheard sore appalde,
  to see that none would heare him.

But as the Swaine amazed stood,
  In this most solemne vaine:
Came Phillida out of the wood,
  And stood before the Swaine.

Whom when the Shepheard did behold,
  He straight began to weepe,
And at the heart he grew a cold,
  To thinke vpon his sheepe.

For wel he knew where came the Queene
  The Shepheard durst not stay,

54

And where he durst not be seene,
  The sheepe must needes away.

To aske her if she saw his flocke,
  Might happen pacience moue:
And haue an answere with a mocke.
  That such demaunders proue.

Yet for because he saw her come,
  Alone out of the wood:
He thought he would not stand as dumbe,
  when speach might do him good.

And therefore falling on his knees,
  To aske but for his sheepe,
He did awake and so did leese,
  The honour of his sleepe.

(51)   *A pleasant sweet song.*

Laid in my restlesse bed,
  In dreame of my desire:
I sawe within my troubled head,
  A heape of thoughts appeare.

And each of them so strange,
  In sight before mine eyes:
That now I sigh and then I smile,
  As cause thereby doth rise.

I see how that the little boy,
  In thought how oft that he:
Doth wish of God to scape the rod,
  a tall yong man to be,

I saw the yong man trauelling,
  From sport to paines opprest:
How he would be a rich olde man,
  To liue and lie at rest.

The olde man too, who seeth,
  His age to drawe on sore:
Would be a little boy againe,
  To liue so long the more.

Whereat I sigh and smile,
  How Nature craues her fee:
From boy to man, from man to boy,
  Would chop and change degree.

(52)   *A Sonet of Time and Pleasure.*

Time is but short, and short the course of time,
Pleasures do passe but as a puffe of winde:
Care hath account to make for euerie crime,
And peace abides but with the setled minde.

Of little paine doth pacience great proceede,
And after sickness, health is daintie sweet:
A friend is best approued at a neede,
And sweet the thought where care & kindnes meet.

Then thinke what comfort doth of kindnes breed,
To know thy sicknesse, sorrow to thy friend:
And let thy faith vpon this fauour feed,
That loue shall liue when death shall haue an end.

And he that liues assured of thy loue,
Prayes for thy life, thy health, and highest hap,
And hopes to see the height of thy behoue,
Lulde in the sweet of Loues desired lap.

Till when, take paines to make thy pillow soft,
And take a nap for Natures better rest:
He liues below that yet doth looke aloft,
And of a friend do not affect the least.

(53)   *Of a Louer is dispaire.*

Though froward fate hath forst my griefe,
And blacke dispaire this deadly paine:
Yet time I trust will bring reliefe,
When loyall faith shall haue her gaine.

Till then the stormes of banisht state,
And penance in his Hermits Cell:
Shall trie her cause of wrongfull hate,
Whose malice lo keepes me in hell,

(54)   *A Sonet of faire womens ficklenesse in loue.*

If women would be faire, and yet not fond,
Or that their loue were firme not fickle still:
I would not wonder that they make men bond,
By seruice long to purchase their good will:
  But when I see how firme these creaturs are,
  I laugh that men forget themselues so farre.

To marke their choise they make and how they chaunge,
How oft from Venus they do cleaue to Pan:
Vnsetled still like haggards vile the raunge,
These gentle birds that flie from man to man:
  Who would not scorn & shake them from his fist.
  And let them go (faire fooles) which way they list.

If for disport we faine and flatter both,
To passe the time when nothing can displease:
And traine them still vnto our subtill oth,
Till wearie of their wits our selues we ease.
  And then we say, when we their fancies trie,
  To play with fooles, oh what a dolt was I.

(55)   *Of the foure Elements.*

The Aire with sweet my sences do delight,
The Earth with flowers doth glad my heauie eie,

57

The Fire with warmth reuiues my dying spirit,
The Water cooles that is too hote and drie:
  The Aire, the Earth, the Water, and the fire,
  All doe me good, what can I more desire.

Oh no, the Aire infected sore I finde,
The Earth, her flowers do wither and decay:
The Fire so whote it doth inflame the minde,
And Water washeth white and all away.
  The Aire, the Earth, Fire, Water, all annoy me.
  How can it be but they must needes destroy me.

Sweete Aire do yet a while thy sweetnesse holde,
Earth, let thy flowers not fall away in prime:
Fire do not burne, my heart is not a colde,
Water, drie vp vntill another time,
  Or Aire, or Earth, Fire, Water, heare my prayer,
  Or slaie me once Fire, Water, Earth, or Aire.

Hearke in the Aire what deadly thunder threateth,
See on the Earth how euery flower falleth,
Oh with the Fire how euery sinewe sweateth.
Oh howe the Water my panting heart appalleth.
  The Aire, the Earth, Fire, Water, all do grieue me.
  Heauens shew your power yet some way to relieue me.

This is not Aire that euerie creature feedeth,
Nor this the Earth where euerie flower groweth:
Nor this the Fire, that cole and bauen breedeth,
Nor this the Water, that both ebth and floweth.
  These Elements are in a worde enclosed,
  Where happie heart hath heauenly rest reposed.

(56)   *Brittons farewell to Hope.*

My Hope farewell, leaue off thy lingring stay,
Nowe yeeld thy selfe as prisoner vnto thrall:
Pricke on thy wings, make now no more delay,

Be set thou art with Enuies furies all.
　Oh Follie flie, fond Fancie leaue thy roome,
　Thou are condemde, Dispaire hath giuen thy doome.

Thy threed whereon thy hope did hang so long,
Dame Enuies rust hath fretted quite in twaine:
And spitefull spite hath gnawne thee to the bone,
That sue thou maist, but all is spent in vaine.
　She is reuert, and giues me still the nay,
　And keepes me like the Spaniell all the day.

When caught I was, I was content to yeeld,
My loue was lim'd and linked to her will:
And prisoner I was brought out of the field,
Of libertie to serue in thraldome still.
　There lost I ioyes, my toiles did then beginne,
　When as I sought a froward heart to winne.

I fought, I sued, I was at becke and bay,
I crept, I kneelde, a heauen it was to please:
I thought my selfe the happiest man that day,
If one faire worde I caught my heart to ease:
　But when that deeds of wordes should then ensue,
　All then was turn'd like vnto Cresseds crew.

Thus do I sue and serue, but all in vaine,
With lingring on my loathsome life in wo:
Thus do I seeke to winne, but losse I gaine,
And for a friend obtaine a spiteful fo:
　Then farewell hope the gaine of my desart,
　Dispaire doth grow within my pensiue heart.
　　　　　　　　F I N I S. N. B. Gent.

NOTES

NOTES

IN THE following Notes the collations with the first edition of *Brittons Bowre of Delights*, 1591, from the 1597 editions of *The Bower* and *The Arbor of amorous Deuises* include all verbal variations and all noteworthy typographical errors, but not wrong-font or (ordinarily) dropped or blurred letters and not faultily spaced words or turned apostrophes. No notice, furthermore, is taken of punctuation. In the case of texts in other books or manuscripts only actual variants in diction, not mere orthographical variations (unless they are, for one reason or another, unusual), are included. The three books named above are referred to throughout as *The Bower* and *The Arbor*, dates being added to distinguish, where it is necessary, the two editions of the former. No comments are made in the Notes on obvious misprints in the 1591 edition, for they can hardly bother any reader who may see this volume.[1] References are to pages and lines of the text.

3. 1–2 *To the Gentlemen Readers*. This preface is repeated almost without change in the 1597 edition, except that the error of *lime or lead* on A2 (not "A3," as the first edition has it) is not mentioned, but is corrected in the text. The "good gentlemen" of line 18 are there called "sweet gentlemen," no notice is taken of Breton's attack (see p. xv) on the first edition, and no indication is given that the book is a reprint. Collations with the 1597 *Bower* follow:

3.18   good] sweet
19   of] for
20   Cauellers, and] cauelling
22   where] if: to] iustlie to

[1] Apart from mere faulty spacing the misprints are usually inverted letters; as, *eud* (18.22) for *end*, *uor* (19.2) for *nor*, *nouce* (32.27) for *nonce*. Of others the most important are *txcellence* (23.5) for *excellence*, *theught* (33.23) for *thought*, *seemt* (46.7) for *seeme*, *Dogenes* (46.16) for *Diogenes*, *setret* (47.7) for *secret*.

    3.23   it] it (I pray you rather: committed] committed, indeed,
    25–26 and . . . lead] *Om.*

The preface is imitated by that in Samuel Pick's thievish *Festum Voluptatis; Or, The Banquet of Pleasure,* 1639.

    5. 2 (No. 1) *Amoris Lachrimae.* In *The Pilgrimage to Paradise,* 1592 (see p. xv, above), Breton acknowledges the authorship of this poem. It is reprinted in *The Bower,* 1597, No. [1], A3–B4ᵛ, with the following variants:

    6. 9   he was] was he
      22   what] whar
      25   and] or
      31   Courteous] Curreous *apparently*
    7. 6   intent] itnent
       8   carried] cartied: full] still
      12   Church] Chureh
      18   lime] line
      25   hath] had
      26   honoured] hovoured
      32   hands] hand
    8. 3   honour] honout
      14   griefe] gtiefe
      19   such] snch
      25   finde] fmde
      26   heart] hearr
      30   heauie] heauir
    9. 5   her] the
       6   crosse] losse
      13   the¹] rhe
  10. 7   no] nv
       8   Death] dearh
       9   the²] rhe
      11   mightest] mightst
      30   consented] contented
      31   the terror] sorrow
  11.16   chuse] chose
      17   griefel] griese
      24   auaile] auailie
      27   **affect]** effect

12. 7   to] no
    11   -aday] -away
13.10   vnhappie] happie
    11   begone] begoo
    13   were, that] wete, thar *apparently*
    16   helpe] holde
14.16   care] cate *apparently*
    26   dolefull] dolefnll
    27   Eagles] Fagles
15. 2   beaten] beated
    12   Neuer] Meuer
    14   neere] neete
    17   and] aud
    21   sight] sigh
    24   Tonitru] Tonitrus
    33   infernale] infernala
16. 3   griefe] gtiefe
    25   warld] world: renowme] renowne

"Amoris Lachrimae" is reprinted from *The Bower* of 1591 in Samuel Butler's *Sidneiana*, pp. 41–53 (Roxburghe Club, 1837), along with John Phillip's (or Phillips's) *The Life and Death of Sir Phillip Sidney, late Lord governour of Flushing,* 1587 (pp. 17–31), and Thomas Churchyard's *The Epitaph of Sir Phillip Sidney Knight, lately Lord Governour of Floshing* [1587?] (pp. 33–39).

Other copies of the poem are preserved in (1) MS. Rawlinson Poet. 85, fols. 27–34ᵛ (attributed to Breton); in (2) MS. Additional 34064, fols. 41–47; and in (3) *The Dr. Farmer Chetham MS.,* ed. A. B. Grosart, Chetham Society, II (1873), 166–177. Collations with these three texts are given below. It should be observed that (3) is entitled "An Epitaph composed by Sʳ Edward Dyer of Sʳ Philip Sidney," and that it omits nine stanzas but adds the two stanzas which form No. 30.

5. 1–4 Amoris lichrimiae [*sic*] on the deathe of .Sʳ. P. Sidneye (1)
    6   time] tymes (1)
    7   most] lefte (1–3)
    8   passe] past (3):   pleasures] pleasure (1, 2)

5. 9 secrets] secret (1–3)
    15 no] not (2, 3)
    16 lost] loose (3):   are] is (3)
    18 the] and (3):   crosse of onely] onlye cross of (1–3)
    22 All] As (1–3):   loue, life] lyfe, loue (1)
    24 lou' de] loued (1, 3)
    26 power] powers (3)
6. 2 had] hath (3)
    4 can] ran (3)
    6 esteemd] esteemed (3)
    8 On] And (2)
    11 a] no (3):   deuoid] voyde (1–3)
    12 ieasts] welth (3)
    13 sometimes] sumtime (2, 3)
    15 things] thinge (1, 3):   himself] he was (2, 3)
    17 secret] fervent (3)
    21 dooth] doe (3)
    23 summe] ffyne (3)
    25 power] honor (3)
    26 thus] soe (3):   did] doth (1):   him] them (3)
    27 could euer] had power to (1):   him] them (3)
    30 in] of (1):   effect] affecte (1–3)
    32 and] Om. (1):   Bountie] beawty (2, 3)
7. 2 peased] prysed (3)
    4 were] was (1–3)
    8 full his] his full (1):   *this stanza and that at line* 14 *are transposed in* (1)
    11 in] on (3):   byding] buildinge (3)
    12 He lou'd] And loued (1):   do] did (1)
    13 are] were (1)
    15 a] the (3)
    16 a] a*n* (1):   eare] or (2, 3):   lome] stone (3)
    17 the] in (1):   seas] sea (3)
    18 depths] depthe (3):   eare] or (2, 3):   lime] line (1–3)
    21 wealth] deathe (1)
    22 begun] began (1)
    23 lou'd] loued (1)
    25 That] And (3)
    26 honoured] honourde (2):   a] one (1)
    27 his ¹] the (1–3):   affection] affections (1)

7.29   light] heighte (3):   of] of his true (3):   direction]
        moste hyghe affections (1)

  30   loued] lovde (2)

  31   resolu'd] resolued (1, 3):   remoued] removde (2)

  32   hands] hand (1–3):   hart] harted (1)

8. 2   where] when (3):   could] woulde (1)

   4   Captaines] captayne (1, 2)

   6   in] of (1)

   9   might] mought (3):   but he] be but (2)

  10   mourne] mourns (1), mone (3)

  11   Nowe] Howe (3)

  13   this] suche (1)

  15   care] case (3)

  17   is but] it is (3)

  20   make] makes (2, 3):   melancholike] melancolie (3)

  21   dooth] dost (?) (1), doe (3):   discontented] disconted (1)

  24   minde] lyfe (1):   ordainde] ordayned (1, 3):   to] for (3)

  26   But] And (3)

  27   liueth] lively (3)

  28   can] maye (1)

  31   some] the (3):   touch] truth (3)

  32   may] my (1)

  33   extremities] extremes (1–3)

9. 4   sit] set (1)

   5   the] his (3):   sittes] satte (3)

   6   on] of (2, 3)

   8   case] state (1)

   9   death and] his deathe's (3)

  10   Sits] Vue (3):   blubbred] blubbered (1, 3)

  13   wailes] waylle (1, 2), wayte (3)

  14   Sits] Sitte (3):   pricking] pikeinge (?) (1), picking (2, 3)

  16   teare] scalde (1)

  17   rend] rent (1):   shriueled] shrivled (1–3)

  18   paine] plume (2)

  19   Among] Amongst (3):   in sunder] a sounder (2, 3)

  20   confesse it is] it seemes to me (1)

  21   oh] I (2, 3):   I²] and (1)

  25   that] thou (3):   knowest] knows (1), knowst (2, 3)

  26   Paint but one] Poynte owte my (3)

  27–11.11 *om. in* (3)

9.30   but] and (1, 2)
  31   where] when (1)
  32   endured] indur'de (1)
10. 2   liue] love *apparently* (2)
   3   this] the (1)
   9   take] make (2)
  11   mightest] myghtste (1, 2)
  12   wearie] cruell (1)
  14   moughtest] myghtst (1), moughtst (2)
  16   killed] kylde (1, 2):   consumed] consum'de (1, 2)
  17   Which] W^th (2):   these worldly] the worlds (1)
  19   it is] thou did'st (1)
  22   draw] drive (2):   in] to (1)
  24   thee] that (2)
  28   doth] do (1, 2)
  32   camst] camest (1)
11. 3   Desired] desirde (2)
   4   quakte] quaked (1)
   5   death now] o death (1)
   6   dost] doest (1)
   7   thine] thy (2)
   8   dost] do (1, 2)
   9   Saint] one (1)
  13   his] her (1–3)
  15   passions] patient (1), passion (2, 3)
  16   would] doth (3)
  17   To] But (1–3)
  19   of] in (1)
  22   by a] else by (1):   I] *Om.* (1):   I might the grace]
         that I might (3)
  24   not] naught (3)
  25   none] no (2), not (3)
  26   my^1] the (2, 3)
  27   thus] so (1):   affect] a facte (1)
  28   As] And (1)
  29   no] not (1–3)
  30   no^1] nor (1)
  33   and] but (1–3)
12. 2   no] not (1)
   3   And . . . nowe] Now none but deathe since (1)

12. 4　alas] alack (1):　　well-away] welladaye (3)
　　6　falne] fallen (1, 3):　　vnto] to (1), into (3)
　　8　of] one (1, 3)
　　9　Let] Tell (3)
　10　ah] o (1, 3):　　gone] ever (3)
　12　Of a] As (1):　　none] never (3)
　14　higher] high (3)
　15　begone] begoms (?) (3)
　16　heauens] heavne (2), heav'ns (3):　　lou'd] loued (1), loue (3)
　17　was ²] Om. (1, 3)
　19　heauen] the heavens (3):　　and] Om. (3):　　heauens]
　　　heauen (1)
　20　Oh] Of (3):　　heauens] heavne (2, 3)
　25　sorrowes such] sorrowe like (3):　　there] yet (1):　　were]
　　　was (2, 3)
　27　should] wold (3)
　31　a] in (3):　　lie] her (3)
　33　It] As (1)
13. 2　horse] horses (1)
　4　thinkes] thincke (3):　　murmure . . . corse] mourninge
　　　on dead corses (1):　　corse] course (3)
　5　the] there (3)
　6　thinkes] thincke (3)
　7　Bids] Bidd (1, 3)
　8　heare the] see a (3):　　13.8–14.11 *follow* 14.12–15.15 *in* (3)
　9　Sound] Singe (1):　　a] la (1):　　mort] most (3)
　10　the'nd] the ende (1, 2), an end (3):　　vnhappie] happy
　　　(1–3)
　12　heare] se (1)
　16　no] not (1)
　17　Not] Nor (1)
　18　When] Wher (1):　　friend] loue (1, 2):　　me] Om. (2)
　20　Yet for] And yet (3)
　21　Which] Who (3):　　did] diddest (1), didst (2, 3):　　no]
　　　not (3)
　22　thy] my (3)
　23　thy] this (3)
　25　I] we (3)
　27　honest] deerest (1)
　28　besides] beside (3)

13.29   sorrow] sorrowes (3):   Shepheards] shephearde (3)
  30   Harke] Heare (1):   blaying] bleatynge (1, 3)
  31   Shepheards] shepperde (2, 3):   towne] tombe (1)
  33   While] And (1):   among] amonngst (1)
14. 2   dooth] doe (3)
   3   That] *Om.* (2):   was] lay (3)
   5   that] how (1)
   7   should] would (1–3)
   9   on] in (1, 3)
  10   the . . . heard] he hard but (3):   the] his (2), the mortall
          (3)
  11   Liu'de] Liued (1)
  12   abandonde] abandoned (1), abandone (3)
  13   Keepes] Keepinge (1), Keepe (3):   the] *Om.* (1):
          vnknowne] not knowne (3)
  15   death] life (3)
  17   griefes] deaths (1):   are] were (1)
  21   casts] cast (1)
  25   And] *Om.* (2):   shriking] screechinge (1), shriching
          (2), screichinge (3)
  26   sing] do singe (2, 3)
  28   and] the (1)
  31   turnde] tornedd (3):   duskie] dustye (3)
  33   fade, fall] fall, fade (1)
15. 2   dried] dride (2), drye (3):   scale] scales (3)
   3   fruite] frutes (1)
   8   beasts] beaste (3):   birds] birde (3)
  10   on] in (1):   euer] neuer (1)
  18   his] the (2):   cracke] wrack (3)
  20   his] all (1)
  21   pitious] wofull (2):   *the line runs in* (3) dyinge in harte
          to see the heavie sighte
  22   Lachrimis] Lacrimae (3)
  26   noble] Nobler (3)
  27   engrauen] ingraued (1)
  28   with] *Om.* (2):   Oh che male] ehe mala (3)
  29   Morte di] male de (3):   di la] della (1)
  30   Morte . . . morte] pieso ehe male (3)
  31   these] this (1), their (2, 3):   Felicita] fælicitae (1)
  32   infernale] infernate (3)

15.33   videre . . . da] vedere morte et non (2):   videre,
         viuere] vider, viuer (3):   morte] male (3)
16. 2-7 *om. in* (3)
    3   is the griefe] greatest is (1):   is²] hath (2)
    4   thoughts] thoughte (1, 2)
    6   paines . . . onely] deadly passions plainlie (2)
    7   Anotamie] Anatomy (1, 2)
    11   can . . . little] neuer yet did (1)
    13   care] cure (2):   my] myne (1)
    16   heale] heate (3):   euery] verie (3):   griefe] yll (2, 3)
    17   And giue the] Beginninge (1):   comfort neuer] never
         Comforte (3)
    18   And] that (3):   where] when (1):   hope] harte (1)
    19   and . . . liue] hathe my loue and him (1)
    21   her] the (1)
    25   warld] worlde (1–3):   renowme] renowne (2, 3):   *after*
         this line (1) *inserts* BRJTON on S. P. S., (2) *inserts* finis./
         Amoris Lachrimæ for the death of/ Sʳ Phillip Sidney.

Some of the foregoing readings — though a number in Grosart's transcript are no doubt incorrect — are especially tempting;
as *no* (6.11), *welth* (6.12; compare *it* in line 1-3), *extremes* (8.33), *I*
(9.21), *With* (10.17), *But* (11.17), *yll* (16.16, required by the rime).

6. 6 *In childish yeares he was esteemd a man.* Compare the
well-known statement of Sir Fulke Greville, Lord Brooke (*Works*,
ed. Grosart, IV [1870], 10), in his biography of Sidney: "though I
lived with him and knew him from a child, yet I never knew him
other than a man: with such staiednesse of mind, lovely, and
familiar gravity, as carried grace and reverence above greater
years. His talk ever of knowledge, and his very play tending to
enrich his mind."

7.26 *he honoured but a starre.* Of course this is a reference
to "Stella," or Lady Rich, on whom see 19.33 n.

12.10 *Oh my loue, ah my loue, &c.* Thomas Nashe (*Works*, ed.
McKerrow, III, 332), in the preface to Sidney's *Astrophel and
Stella*, utters a slur at *The Bower* (see p. xxiv, above) and, in a
passage not hitherto identified goes on to ridicule the present

line: "my stile is somewhat heauie gated, and cannot daunce trip and goe so liuely, with oh my loue, ah my loue, all my loues gone, as other Sheepheards that haue beene fooles in the Morris time out of minde." Compare also Ben Jonson, *The Case Is Altered*, 1597, IV. vii (ed. W. E. Selin, 1917, p. 65):

> *Juniper.* Yea? so nimble in your D*ilemma's*, and your *Hiperbole's* Hay my loue? O my loue, at the first sight: By the masse.
> *Onion.* O how she skudded, O sweet scud, how she tripped, O deli-cate trip and goe.

13.31   *Shepheards.* The reading should be *Shepherd*, as in the MSS.

15.16   *First comes the brother, &c.* Robert Sidney, later the Earl of Leicester (1563–1626), acted as chief mourner at his brother's funeral.

28–33   .*The straungers come, &c.* The following corrections should be made in the Italian tags: *mala* (28), *de* (29), *più* (30), *Felicità* (31), *vedere* (33). Line 33 is not clear, but it was no doubt intended to mean, "fit to see death, not to live." Professor C. H. Grandgent kindly gives me the following metrical translation:

> The straungers come with *Good luck perisheth*,
> The seruants come with *Death of liuelihood*,
> The secret friends with *Death outdoing Death*,
> And all with these *Delight is fled for good:*
> Nowe for my selfe, *O pains of hell*,
> *To look on death were mine, not here to dwell.*

17. 2   (No. 2) *A pleasant Poem.* Reprinted, without variants, in *The Bower*, 1597, No. [2], C1. As a mere guess, this stilted, arti-ficial poem may be in honor of Anne Parker, daughter of the Sussex soldier Sir Nicholas Parker (1547–1619). In 1602 she mar-ried Adrian Moore, one of the adventurers of the Virginia Com-pany.

14   (No. 3) *Another.* Reprinted in *The Bower*, 1597, No. [3], C1, with the roman capital in line 17 misprinted *F* (instead of

E), thus ruining the acrostic. The poem was written in honor of, not by, Elizabeth Trentham, daughter of Thomas Trentham, of Rocester Priory, Staffordshire. In 1591 she became the second wife of Edward de Vere, seventeenth Earl of Oxford, by whom she was the mother of Henry, the eighteenth earl; and she was buried at Hackney on January 3, 1613 (see Violet A. Wilson, *Queen Elizabeth's Maids of Honour*, 1922, pp. 134, 180). Elizabeth Trentham was a maid of honor at least as early as April 5, 1582, the date on which she, with Elizabeth Garret of No. 4 and others, was mentioned in a letter written by J. Farnham to Roger Manners (*Historical Manuscripts Commission. Twelfth Report, Appendix, Part IV* [Rutland MSS., I, 134]): "Mrs. Trentham is as fair, Mrs. Edgcombe as modest, Mrs. Radcliff as comely, and Mrs. Garrat as jolly as ever." In 1588/9 the queen gave her, Anne Hopton of No. 43, and Mistresses Mackwilliams, Southwell, and Cavendish (three other maids of honor who are celebrated in *The Arbor*) New Year's gifts of gilt plate (John Nichols, *The Progresses and Public Processions of Queen Elizabeth*, III [1823], 20).

The first countess of Edward de Vere died in 1588. It would be pleasant if one could prove that the Earl of Oxford wrote this poem in praise of his future second wife. He was a poet of great reputation — so great that various misguided persons to-day believe him to have been Shakespeare. Whoever the author, he manages in lines 20–22 to pay a graceful and no doubt an acceptable compliment to the "heauenly Queene" Elizabeth.

17.24 (No. 4) *Another*. Reprinted, without variants, in *The Bower*, 1597, No. [4], C1. This frigid poem was probably written in praise of (not by) Elizabeth Garret (see also the notes to No. 3), who became a maid of honor in 1571. On May 14, 1571, George Delves wrote to the Earl of Rutland (*Historical Manuscripts Commission. Twelfth Report, Appendix, Part IV* [Rutland MSS., I, 92–93]): "Hennigam (Hennyngham?) never looked so well as since she tasted the quintessence out of the long-necked bottle. She keeps her place in Court, but not as maid. In her room came

Mr. Garratt's daughter." Mistress Garret is mentioned again as a maid of honor in 1577/8 (John Nichols, *The Progresses and Public Processions of Queen Elizabeth*, II [1823], 88).

18. 2 (No. 5) *A sweete Pastorall*. Reprinted in *The Bower*, 1597, No. [5], C1ᵛ, with the following variants:

18.	5	Sweet] Sweer:	knowst] knowest
	10	colours] colour	
	18	to] ro	
	19	therefore] rherefore	

A copy in MS. Additional 34064, fols. 2ᵛ–3, entitled "A pastorall," has the following variants:

18.	5	be gone] begon:	knowst] seest
	12	they] to	
	13	Philomele] Philomene	
	17	kill] byll	
	19	knowst] knowest	

The poem was reprinted (from the 1597 edition) in *England's Helicon*, 1600, E4ᵛ–F1ᵛ, with the signature "N. Breton": in that reprint (as in the foregoing manuscript) the long lines are broken in two, thus making the internal rime obvious. In *Reliques of Ancient English Poetry*, 1765 (ed. H. B. Wheatley, III [1887], 80–81), Bishop Percy printed "A sweete Pastorall" from a manuscript "improved by a more perfect copy in *England's Helicon*." The diction strongly suggests Breton's authorship.

23 (No. 6) *A Sonet*. The omission of this poem, as well as Nos. 7–9, from the 1597 editions of both *The Bower* and *The Arbor* is hard to explain. An untitled copy in MS. Additional 34064, fols. 3–3ᵛ, has the following variants:

18.25	mate] make
27	hir] *Om.*
34	withered] witherde
19. 8	their ¹, ²] her
9	neuer do me] doe me neuer

19.11 it] ᵗ⁄ᵧ
14 sadb] sobde

The style and diction (compare especially the "bird-lists" with
14.24–29 and 18.11–14) suggest Breton's authorship.

19.14 *My tree of true delight, is sabd with sorrow so.* Possibly
sabd is an error for *sapp'd*, but probably (as the manuscript reading suggests) it should be *sobb'd*, meaning "soaked." The *New
English Dictionary* gives its earliest examples of *sobbed* in that
sense from 1625 and 1658, the second being John Evelyn's "When
the tree being sobb'd and wet, swells the wood, and loosens the
fruit."

18 (No. 7) *A Poem.* See the comments on No. 6. Two
untitled copies in MS. Additional 34064, fols. 3ᵛ (*A*), 26 (*B*), have
the following variants:

19.19 the] thy *B*: my] the *A*, thy *B*
20 seruāts] servant *B*: but] And *B*
21 speake but] tell her *B*
24 That shee] Yf thow *B*: loue] har *B*
25 that] ye *B*
27 to] so *AB*: strange] strand *B*
31 fairest] soerest *B*
32 flame] fedes *B*: dies] dieth *B*

A partial copy, without a title, is preserved in MS. Egerton 2230,
fols. 29–28ᵛ, with the following variants:

19.19 whereas my] Where my fayre
20 but] And
21 speake but] whisper
22 not . . . helpe] send me nott reliefe
23 Not . . . but] Perhaps shee doth not know Or
24 looke] thinke
25 knowes it not] doth not know
27–32 *Om.*

33 (No. 8) *A Poem.* See the comments on No. 6. This stiff

and mechanical poem is not known to be preserved elsewhere. The printer failed to observe that the initial letters spell the acrostic "Penelope Rich." Penelope Devereux, the Stella of Sidney's sonnets (cf. 7.26 n.), is supposed to have become Lady Rich in 1581. Her praises were sung also by Richard Barnfield, Bartholomew Yong, Henry Constable, Alexander Craig, and John Davies of Hereford; but in 1591 the acrostic-poem would probably have suggested only Sidney's authorship, especially since so much of the volume is definitely connected with Sidney. For a popular and mildly interesting account of Stella, one might consult Maud Stepney Rawson's *Penelope Rich and her Circle* (1911).

20. 2 *glaces growe*. Rime requires *grewe*. Perhaps *glaces* (literally *ices*) refers to snow-covered hills, but it may be a misprint for *graces*.

12 (No. 9) *A Pastorall*. See the comments on No. 6.

14 *Mine eyes, &c.* Read *Mine ears*. Evidently a line with a rime-word for *heart* and dealing with the tongue and the hand has been omitted here. As lines 14–15 stand, they are meaningless.

24 (No. 10) *A Poem*. Perhaps this poem was omitted from *The Arbor* and *The Bower* of 1597 because another version of it had meanwhile appeared in *The Phoenix Nest*, 1593, K3-K3^v, and because it was generally thought to be the composition of Sir Walter Raleigh. It is one of the most popular Elizabethan lyrics. Other versions will be found in Alfonso Ferrabosco's *Ayres*, 1609, B1 (cf. E. H. Fellowes, *English Madrigal Verse*, p. 460); in *To day a man, To morrow none: Or, Sir VValter Ravvleighs Farevvell to his Lady*, 1644; in Nicholas Laniere's *Select Musicall Ayres and Dialogues*, 1653 (with music); in Arthur Clifford's *Tixall Poetry*, 1813, pp. 115–116 (from a manuscript); and in E. F. Rimbault's *A Little Book of Songs and Ballads, gathered from Ancient Musick Books*, 1851, pp. 98–100 (from Laniere). Copies are preserved, furthermore, in MS. Harleian 6910, fol. 139^v (*ca.* 1596); MS. Additional 38823, fol. 58^v (Sir Edward Hoby's commonplace-book, *ca.* 1596), under the heading "Incerti Authoris"; John Harington's manu-

script (*ca.* 1560) as represented by a modern copy (transcribed by
G. F. Nott) in MS. Additional 28635, fol. 86^v; MS. Rawlinson
Poet. 85, fol. 25^v, of the early seventeenth century. For collations of these texts see my edition of *The Phoenix Nest* (1931),
pp. 168–169.

John Hannah accepts the poem as Raleigh's, reprinting it from
The Phoenix Nest in *The Poems of Sir Walter Raleigh . . . and Other
Courtly Poets*, 1875, 1892, pp. 12–13, as does Raleigh's most recent
(1929) editor, Agnes M. C. Latham, p. 35. Thomas Park (editing *The Phoenix Nest* in 1814) and Rimbault pointed out references
to the poem by Phineas Fletcher (*Poetical Works*, ed. F. S. Boas, II
[1909], 249–250), Izaac Walton (*The Complete Angler*, 1653, I. v,
ed. Gough and Balston, 1915, p. 121 n.), Samuel Butler (*Hudibras*,
I. ii. 1168), Samuel Pepys (*Diary*, February 12, 1667), Roger
North (*Lives*, II [1826], 12). In a spurious letter printed by Collier
in *Archaeologia*, XXXIV [1851], 161–162, two lines of the poem
are quoted in reference to Raleigh himself.

No. 10 is (as I pointed out in *The* [London] *Times Literary
Supplement*, December 12, 1929, p. 1058) a felicitous translation
(with its last two lines original) of Philippe Desportes's *Amours de
Diane*, II. viii (*Œuvres*, ed. Michiels, p. 71):

> Je me veux rendre hermite et faire penitence
> De l'erreur de mes yeux pleins de temerité,
> Dressant mon hermitage en un lieu deserté,
> Dont nul autre qu' Amour n'aura la connoissance.
>   D'ennuis et de douleurs je feray ma pitance,
> Mon bruvage de pleurs; et, par l'obscurité,
> Le feu qui m'ard le cœur servira de clairté
> Et me consommera pour punir mon offance.
>   Un long habit de gris le corps me couvrira,
> Mon tardif repentir sur mon front se lira,
> Et le poignant regret qui tenaille mon ame.
>   D'un espoir languissant mon baston je feray,
> Et tousjours, pour prier, devant mes yeux j'auray
> La peinture d'Amour et celle de ma dame.

How felicitous this translation really is can best be appreciated by comparing it with an independent rendering made by Thomas Lodge in *Scillaes Metamorphosis*, 1589, E4–E4ᵛ (pp. 43–44, *Complete Works*, ed. Hunterian Club, vol. I), or with another (headed "Jncerti Authoris") in MS. Additional 38823, fol. 8. Much like No. 10, and perhaps imitated from it or from Desportes, is No. 16.

21. 2 *A gowne of griefe*. Read *A gowne of gray*, as in Desportes and *The Phoenix Nest*. Probably the author originally wrote *griefe* (French *gris*).

8 (No. 11) *Of his Mistresse loue*. The title, evidently made by the printer or his "corrector" after a hasty glance at line 10, is incorrect: it should be "Of his Mistress, Love, and Diana." The poem is reprinted in *The Arbor*, 1597, No. [35], F1, with the following variants:

21. 9   strength] sttength
    10   Mistresse Loue] Mistresse, Laue
    11   Ladies] Ladier
    13   Loue] Lone
    20   my] me

Grosart (Breton, I, lxvi) observed that No. 11 is a translation of Philippe Desportes's *Amours de Diane*, I. xv (*Œuvres*, ed. Michiels, p. 19):

> Un jour l'aveugle Amour, Diane et ma maistresse,
> Ne pouvans s'accorder de leur dexterité,
> S'essayerent de l'arc à un but limité,
> Et mirent pour le prix leur plus belle richesse.
>   Amour gaigea son arc, et la chaste deesse
> Qui commande aux forests, sa divine beauté;
> Ma maistresse gaigea sa fiere cruauté,
> Qui me fait consommer en mortelle tristesse.
>   Las! ma dame gaigna, remportant pour guerdon
> La beauté de Diane et l'arc de Cupidon,
> Et la dure impitié dont son ame est couverte.
>   Pour essayer ses traits, elle a perçé mon cœur;
> Sa beauté m'esbloüit, je meurs par sa rigueur:
> Ainsi sur moy, chétif, tombe toute la perte.

He likewise points out the following paraphrase of Desportes in Bartholomew Griffin's *Fidessa*, 1596 (ed. Grosart, p. 57):

> Three play-fellowes (such three were neuer seene
>   In *Venus* court) vpon a summers day,
> Met altogether on a pleasant greene,
>   Intending at some pretie game to play.
> They *Dian, Cupid,* and *Fidessa* were:
>   Their wager, beautie, bow, and crueltie:
> The conqueresse the stakes away did beare,
>   Whose fortune then it was to winne all three.
> *Fidessa,* which doth these as weapons vse,
>   To make the greatest heart her will obay:
> And yet the most obedient to refuse,
>   As hauing power poore louers to betray.
> With these she wounds, she heales, giues life and death:
> More power hath none that liues by mortall breath.

In Gaspar Gil Polo's sequel to Montemayor, *La Diana Enamorada* (see Bartholomew Yong's *Diana*, 1598, p. 495), the last poem is introduced by Olympius as "a pretie Sonnet, made of the skill, beautie, and cruelty of that Shepherdesse [Argia], fayning a challenge and contention betweene her, the Goddesse *Diana* and *Cupid*, whether of them three should shoote best, a fine and delicate conceit, which sometimes to delight me, I euer haue by hart." The sonnet runs as follows:

> Diana, Loue, *and my faire* Shepherdesse,
>   *Did in the field their chiefest cunning trie,*
>   *By shooting arrowes at a tree neere by,*
> *Whose barke a painted hart did there expresse:*
> Diana *stakes her beautie mercilesse,*
>   Cupid *his bowe,* Argia *her libertie*:
>   *Who shewed in her shot a quicker eie,*
> *A better grace, more courage, and successe:*
> *And so did she* Dianas *beautie win,*
>   *And* Cupids *weapons, by which conquer'd prize*
> *So faire and cruell she hath euer bin,*
>   *That her sweete figure from my wearied eies,*

And from my painfull hart her cruell bowe
Haue stolne my life and freedome long agoe.

The author adds that "This Sonnet was maruellous delightfull" to all the shepherds and shepherdesses, who "discoursed of euery particular part and matter of it."

    21.21 *Vigor.* Read *Rigor.*

    23 (No. 12) *Of a discontented minde.* Reprinted in *The Arbor*, 1597, No. [36], F1, with the following variants:

    21.24 each] teach
      25 that] rhat
      32 can once] *Om.*

An untitled copy in MS. Additional 34064, fol. 5ᵛ, varies only in having *a harte* for *an heart* (line 27). It follows the reading of *The Bower* at 21.32.

    22. 2 (No. 13) *Of his Mistresse beautie.* Reprinted in *The Arbor*, 1597, No. [37], F1–F1ᵛ, with the following variants:

    22. 3 distraught] distaught
     14 mad] made
     29 those] these

An untitled copy in MS. Additional 34064, fols. 5ᵛ–6, varies in the following particulars:

    22. 3 distraught] be strought
     16 doth] doe
     21 these] those
     25 And] *Om.*
     27 where] when: among] amongst
     29 among those] amongst these
     30 our wits] all witt
     33 A mazed] Amazed

The diction and the subject-matter of this poem are suggestive of No. 14. Compare especially lines 11 and 13 with 22.37 and 23.7. But the play upon *eyes*, *hearts*, and *hands* occurs also in Nos. 9 and 48. It seems to me unlikely that Breton wrote any of the four.

22.35   (No. 14) *A Sonet.* Reprinted in *The Arbor*, 1597, No. [38], F1ᵛ–F2, with *power* for *powers* (line 10). An untitled copy in MS. Additional 34064, fol. 7ᵛ, varies as follows:

23.   7   hold] holdes
     9   shewe] shewes
   14   minde] wise

Other copies will be found in *The Phoenix Nest*, 1593, L1ᵛ–L2, and in MS. Rawlinson Poet. 85, fol. 24ᵛ. No. 14 bears a considerable resemblance to another poem in *The Phoenix Nest* (K2ᵛ–K3), beginning "Those eies which set my fancie on a fire," and translated from Desportes's *Amours de Diane*, I. 11 (*Œuvres*, ed. Michiels, p. 17). It may itself be an adaptation of Desportes.

23.14   *the minde.* Rime requires *the wise*, as in the manuscript cited above.

18   (No. 15) *A pastorall of Phillis and Coridon.* Reprinted in *The Arbor*, 1597, No. [39], F2–F2ᵛ, with the following variants:

23.28   shepheards] shepheatds
24.   4   fact] face

The foregoing reading at 24.4 should be adopted. It is repeated in an untitled copy in MS. Additional 34064, fols. 8–8ᵛ, which also changes *Corridon* (24.11) to *Choridon*, and adds a new final stanza:

> Make him liue that dying longe
>   neuer durst for comfort seeke
> Thow shalte heare so sweete a songe
>   neuer Shepperde sounge the like.

The poem was reprinted (probably from *The Arbor* of 1597) in *England's Helicon*, 1600, E2ᵛ–E3, with the signature "N. Breton," who very likely *was* the author. Samuel Pick included it as of his own composition in *Festum Voluptatis; Or, The Banquet of Pleasure*, 1639, D2–D2ᵛ, making changes as follows:

23.20   daintie] gentle
   32   And] That

24. 4   fact] face
     8   yet] but
    15   life] live

The reading at 24.4 suggests that Pick plundered *The Arbor* of 1597; his readings at 23.32 and 24.4, but none of the others, are likewise in *England's Helicon*, which also has *euer eye did yet* for *did euer eye* (line 26). An enlarged and a somewhat changed version of No. 15 was printed as a broadside ballad, "The Shepheard's Delight. To the tune of *Frog Galliard*," about 1620 (R. H. Evans, *Old Ballads, Historical and Narrative*, I [1810], 113–114; William Chappell, *The Roxburghe Ballads*, II [1874], 526–529). Chappell (without identifying the author) remarks that the tune was composed by John Dowland and will be found in *Popular Music of the Olden Time*, I, 127, and that another version of the ballad occurs in *The New Academy of Complements*, 1713 (which I have not seen).

24.16   (No. 16) *The complaint of a forsaken Louer*. Reprinted in *The Arbor*, 1597, No. [40], F2ᵛ, with the following variants:

24.16   forsaken] sorsaken
    17   seeke] secke
    21   hollow] hallow
    30   louers] Loners

An untitled copy in MS. Additional 34064, fol. 18, has no variants. This poem closely resembles No. 10 (see 20.24 n.) in subject-matter.

29   *engraue vpon my tombe.* See 25.17.

31   (No. 17) *A prettie Fancie*. Reprinted, without variants, in *The Arbor*, 1597, No. [41], F2ᵛ. An untitled copy in MS. Additional 34064, fol. 17, corrects *Item* (25.2) to *Jem*, and changes the second *the* in 25.5 to *and*.

25. 6   (No. 18) *An Epitaph on the death of a noble Gentleman*. Reprinted in *The Arbor*, 1597, No. [42], F3–F4, with the following variants:

25.16   and] ank
   22   reach] teach
   26   vertues] vertue
   32   the] rhe
   33   his ¹] is
26.18   since] sence
   25   commendation] commendations
   34   is] ls *apparently*

An untitled copy in MS. Additional 34064, fols. 14–15, has the following variants:

25.17   fields] feilde
   20   in] on
   33   Valor] valure
26.12   may] might
   18   since] sence
   31   sighes] sightes
   32   dolefull] wofull
   37   in] *Om.*
27. 3   booke (?)] bookes
    7   friends] freinde
    9   lou'de] loved
   11   said] saie
   16   Valor] valure
   17   honor] sorrow

The foregoing readings for 27.11 and 27.17 should no doubt be adopted. The "noble Gentleman" of the title is, of course, Sidney. The poem certainly sounds like Breton's work: in any case, it imitates closely his No. 1.

25. 8 *Sorrow come sit thee downe.* Commentators have apparently failed to observe that this phrase is twice quoted in *Love's Labour's Lost*, I. i. 316–317, IV. iii. 4–6, "Affliction may one day smile again; and till then, sit thee down, sorrow!" "Well, set thee down, sorrow! for so they say the fool said, and so say I, and I the fool."

14 *Poets lay downe your pennes.* See 27.27 n.

25.23 *Whose workes are extant to the worlde.* The *Arcadia* had
been published in 1590, the *Astrophel and Stella* in 1591.

26.38 *Oxford, Cambridge.* A reference to the volumes of elegies
edited by William Gager and John Lhuyd at Oxford, by Alexander
Neville at Cambridge.

27. 3 *booke* (?). Rime requires *bookes*.

7 *The father.* Sir Henry Sidney had died on May 5, 1586,
five months before his son Philip.

21 (No. 19) *The summe of the former in foure lines.* Reprinted, without variants, in *The Arbor*, 1597, No. [43], F4. A
copy in MS. Additional 34064, fol. 15, has *valure* for *Valor* (line
22). The poem is a sort of "envoy" to No. 18, and one author —
perhaps Breton — must have written both No. 18 and No. 19.

26 (No. 20) *In the praise of his Mistresse.* Reprinted in *The
Arbor*, 1597, No. [44], F4–F4ᵛ, with the following variants:

27.28 or] ot
28.15 the ¹] tbe
17 out] our: vnto] vnroo
18 For] Foe
21 where both] what doth
25 the] rhe

An untitled copy in MS. Additional 34064, fol. 19, varies as follows:

27.34 To] do
35 and] an
28. 9 When] Wher
15 may] shall
17 stuffe] stuffes
18 thou wert] there were
19 euerie ¹, ²] anie
22 where] when: Nature] natures

The style and diction suggest Breton's authorship.

27 *Poets lay downe your pennes.* This exact phraseology
occurs in the preceding poem at 25.14.

28.26   (No. 21) *Of Truth and Loue.* Reprinted in *The Bower*, 1597, No. [6], C1ᵛ–C2, with the following variants:

28.26   *Title changed to* Of Trueth, Wisdome, Vertue and Loue
   30   in his] is the
   34   dyes] lyes
29. 5   Honour] Vertue
    6   vouchsafe] vouchafe

A copy entitled "Againe vpon the same subiect" in MS. Additional 34064, fol. 20, varies as follows:

28.27   in] is
   32   where] when
   33   too small] to sale

The foregoing reading at 28.33 should be adopted.

29. 8   (No. 22) *Rare newes.* Reprinted, without variants, in *The Bower*, 1597, No. [7], C2.

    23   (No. 23) *Of a wearie life.* Reprinted, without variants, in *The Bower*, 1597, No. [8], C2–C2ᵛ. Another copy, forming the conclusion to a poem of six stanzas (beginning "Some men will saie there is a kinde of muse"), in MS. Additional 34064, fols. 20ᵛ–21ᵛ (a third copy is in MS. Harleian 7392, fols. 76ᵛ–77), varies as follows:

29.25   dire] deepe
   32   That] The
30. 2   but that] that but
    4   abusde] abused
    6   Reason] reasons
    8   his] the
   10   But hold] Behold
   13   t'is] till

The last three stanzas (30.4–21) appear as stanzas 3, 5, 6 in "A most excellent passion set downe *by N. B. Gent.*", a poem in *The Phoenix Nest*, 1593, I4–K1, with the following variants:

30. 4   abusde] abused

30. 6   himselfe refusde] hir selfe refused
    8   his] the
   10   But hold] Behold
   11   torment] torments
   13   As] That
   21   will ¹, ²] would

The style and diction of No. 23 strongly suggest Breton's author-ship. Compare especially 30.10–21 with 8.11–22.

    30.16–21   *Loe thus I liue, &c.* The rhetorical device in these lines — a favorite of Breton's, who uses it at 10.26–28 and 45.24–27 — is described by the author of *The Arte of English Poesie*, 1589 (ed. Edward Arber, p. 216), as "the *marching figure*, for after the first steppe all the rest proceede by double the space, and so in our speach one word proceedes double to the first that was spoken, and goeth as it were by strides or paces; it may aswell be called the *clyming* figure, for *Clymax* is as much to say as a ladder."

    22   (No. 24) *Of his vnhappie state of life.* Reprinted in *The Bower*, 1597, No. [9], C2ᵛ–C3, with the following variants:

30.26   griefes] griefe
   34   my ¹] may
31. 2   constant] eonstant *apparently*
    7   these] those

    31. 8–9   *Then by this riuall of my such dispise, &c.* Professor Kittredge emends *by* to *if* and suggests that the lines mean: "Then if this sharer with me in such contempt as I have described," etc.

    14   (No. 25) *His complaint against Loue and Fortune.* Re-printed in *The Bower*, 1597, No. [10], C3–C3ᵛ, with *most* (3.23) omitted and *thus* (32.9) changed to *this*. An untitled copy in MS. Additional 34064, fols. 22–22ᵛ, has the following variants:

31.16   plague] plunge
   17   To] The
   23   loued] lovde
   25   remoued] removde
   36   comfort] comfortes

32. 3   Where] When
    7   consumed] consumde

The diction of the poem suggests Breton's authorship, as do also the trisyllabic rimes in *me* at 31.35–36, 32.2–3. With the latter compare 8.9–10, 8.33 and 9.2, 10.24–25, 11.4–5, 10–11, 16–17, 12.14–15, etc.

32.12   (No. 26) *In the praise of his Penelope.* Reprinted in *The Bower*, 1597, No. [11], C3ᵛ–C4, with the misprint *constaut* (33.5). An untitled copy in MS. Additional 34064, fol. 22ᵛ, has the following variants:

32.16   Orlandos] Orlantos *apparently*
    23   loudly] lewdly
    26   voice] vaine
    27   for the] the the

The foregoing readings for 32.23 and 32.26 should be adopted.

    16   *Ariosto, Orlandos fit.* Angelica (cf. 32.34, 33.8), the Indian queen, is a leading character in Ariosto's *Orlando Furioso*. The argument to Sir John Harington's translation, 1591, I. 5 (1634 ed., p. 1), runs:

> *Orlando* who long time had loved deare,
>   *Angelica* the faire: and for her sake,
> About the world, in nations far and neare,
>   Did high attempts performe and undertake.

After Orlando's madness Angelica woos and weds the page Medore.

    32   *she whom some a Goddesse faine.* Possibly Venus or Helen.

33.10   (No. 27) *A Poem.* Reprinted in *The Bower*, 1597, No. [12], C4, with the following variants:

33.20   thine] thy
    24   the dead] therein

An untitled copy in MS. Additional 34064, fol. 25, has the following variants:

33.11   those] thes
   17   not] no
   18   to] *Om.*:   conquest of] conquer for
   21   thy] thine: lock] looke: thought] thoughtes
   24   dead] deede: thee of] *Om.*

33.16   *And if a worde go vnawares, &c.* Compare Horace, *De
Arte Poetica*, line 390, "nescit vox missa reverti," and *Epistles*, I.
xviii. 71, "et semel emissum volat irrevocabile verbum."

   25   (No. 28) *A Poem.* Reprinted in *The Bower*, 1597, No.
[13], C4–C4ᵛ, with *the* (line 26) misprinted *rhe* and *to* (line 29) re-
placed by *and*. An untitled copy in MS. Additional 34064, fol.
25ᵛ, substitutes *Ph:* for *Phillip* (line 31). The initial letters of the
lines form the acrostic "Philip Philip" (that is, Sidney): no indication of that fact is given by the printer, although in the 1597 edition he doubles (as in Nos. 2–4) some of these initials, "PHIL P
PHI." No. 28 seems to have been imitated from Breton's *Amoris
Lachrimae*, especially 8.23–33, 9.2–8. Compare, for example, lines
32, 33, with 9.3–4.

   34. 5   (No. 29) *A Poem.* Reprinted, without variants, in *The
Bower*, 1597, No. [14], C4ᵛ. The initial letters of the lines form the
acrostic "Philip" (Sidney), as is shown by double letters in the
1597 edition. Apparently No. 29 is merely a third stanza of No.
28, not a separate poem. Indeed it seems not unlikely that Nos.
28, 29, 30 were originally one poem, which Jones for reasons of his
own split into three.

   12   (No. 30) *A Poem.* Reprinted in *The Bower*, 1597, No.
[15], C4ᵛ, with *honors* (line 16) changed to *honour*. The initial
letters of the lines form the acrostic "Philip Sidney," as is shown
in the 1597 edition by double letters (that for *E* at 34.23 being in a
wrong font and blurred beyond recognition, though probably a
lower-case *e*, *a*, or *s*). A second (untitled) copy in MS. Additional
34064, fol. 25, has the following variants:

34.15   in] is
  18   pleased] pleasde
  24   is] hathe

A third copy in *The Dr. Farmer Chetham MS.* (ed. Grosart, II, 176–177), where it forms the conclusion to No. 1 (see the discussion in the notes to 5.2), has the following variants:

34.15   discretion tride] direction tryed
  16   Loue . . . life] life . . . love: honors] hono^r
  19   oh] or
  21   gifts] gueste: on] and
  22   No] in: of] from
  23   End] And: hath] haue
  24   is] hath

34.19–20 *Seeke all the world, &c.* According to the rime-scheme these lines should be transposed.

  25 (No. 31) *Vpon a scoffing laughter giuen by a Gentlewoman.* Reprinted in *The Bower*, 1597, No. [16], C4^v–D1, with the following variants:

34.32   Monkies] Moonkies
  33   a] *Om.*

Evidently from one of the editions of *The Bower* Samuel Pick lifted this poem and included it in his *Festum Voluptatis; Or, The Banquet of Pleasure*, 1639, C2^v–C3, as an original composition. Pick changed only *within a* (35.9) to *within the*.

  35.13 (No. 32) *A sweete contention betweene Loue, his Mistresse, and Bewtie.* The title (cf. the notes to No. 11) is incorrect, as only two figures, Love and the Mistress, "contend." The poem is reprinted in *The Bower*, 1597, No. [17], D1, with the following variants:

35.19   my] me
  32   little] lirtle *apparently*
  35   trumpet sounds] trumpets sound

35.19 *my pearing sence.* Professor Kittredge explains the phrase as "my sense that gazed intensely at her, that had eyes only for her."

36. 2 (No. 33) *A Sonet to the tune of a hone a hone.* Reprinted in *The Bower*, 1597, No. [18], D1ᵛ, with *endlesse* (line 16) changed to *inward*, and *an* (line 30) to *and*. No. 33 was obviously a broadside ballad. *O hone* was an Irish lamentation: for comments on a tune, apparently later than 1591, so named, see Chappell's *Popular Music of the Olden Time*, I, 369–370.

37. 2 (No. 34) *In commendation of the maides of Honour.* Reprinted in *The Bower*, 1597, No. [19], D2, with *creature* (line 8) changed to *treasure*, and *Chose* (line 9) to *Choose*. In spite of the title, which in the author's manuscript certainly must have had the singular *maid* instead of the plural *maides*, Jones failed (in both editions) to notice that the initial letters of the verses spell the acrostic "Frauncis Haward." Frances was the daughter of Thomas Howard, Viscount Howard of Bindon (1528?–1583), who was the second son of Thomas Howard, third Duke of Norfolk and younger brother of the poet Surrey (according to the *Dictionary of National Biography* and Violet A. Wilson, *Queen Elizabeth's Maids of Honour*, 1922, p. 176 n. Vicary Gibbs, *The Complete Peerage*, VI [1926], 506 [as well as Mrs. Wilson, pp. 10, 76], makes her out to have been the daughter of William Howard, first Baron Effingham). She is referred to as a maid of honor in a letter written by George Delves to the Earl of Rutland on May 14, 1571 (*Historical Manuscripts Commission. Twelfth Report, Appendix, Part IV* [Rutland MSS., I, 93]). Mrs. Wilson, with considerable vagueness in dates (pp. 83, 96–99), points out that Lady Howard's persistent suitor was Thomas Coningsby, of Hampton Court, Herefordshire, while she was in love with the Earl of Leicester, who, however, finally married Douglas Howard, the widowed Lady Sheffield (whom Mrs. Wilson wrongly describes as the sister of Frances); that she became keeper of the queen's jewels, succeeding Blanche Parry (p. 132); and that she finally flouted Coningsby to marry

the Earl of Hertford with "the joyful will and good liking of the
Queen" (pp. 107, 143). Frances was married three times: to
Henry Pranell, a wine merchant, who died about 1600; to Sir
Edward Seymour, Earl of Hertford (1539?-1621), on May 27,
1601; to Ludovick Stuart, second Duke of Lennox and Duke of
Richmond (1574-1624). She died in October, 1639, at the age of
sixty-three, and was buried beside her last husband in West-
minster Abbey. For portraits of her see *The Third Annual Volume
of the Walpole Society*, 1914, plate XXX, and p. 39. Some account
of her life is given also in *Archaeologia Cantiana*, XI, 225-250.

37.18   (No. 35) *Diana virgin, her complaint to the Goddesse
Diana.* Reprinted in *The Bower*, 1597, No. [20], D2-D2ᵛ, with the
following variants:

37.20	sweet]	swtet
31	heart]	hurt
38. 6	thoughts]	*Last* t *inverted*
7	found]	fouud
11	wrought]	wrough,

The foregoing reading at 37.31 must be adopted.

38. 6 *In heauenly thoughts hath Reason no remorce.* Apparently a reminiscence of Virgil's *Aeneid*, I. 11, "Tantaene animis
caelestibus irae?"

16   (No. 36) *Brittons vision of Cupids complaint, &c.* Reprinted in *The Bower*, 1597, No. [21], D2ᵛ-D4ᵛ, with the following
variants:

38.18	thoughts]	tboughts
28	he]	she
33	to]	ro
39. 4	I]	*Blurred and unreadable*
22	fauoured]	fauonred
23	matter]	marter
40. 8	that]	the
14	Mars ²]	Marss
22	slugguish]	sluggish

41. 3   When] Wnat
    12   will] well
    14   whine] whi
    29   pedegree] petegree
    33   Fed] For
42. 8   Lodge] Lodgde
    19   conceites] conceite
    24   op] vp

Breton was fond of dream-poems, and there is no reason to doubt that No. 36 is his work. Here Cupid complains (39.22) of the "ill fauoured filthie theefe," Vulcan, who pretends to be his father, and insists (41.24–25), "*Vulcans* sonne I know I cannot be, *Mars* was the man." Mythology supports Breton's Cupid, for Eros (the Greek name for Cupid) is usually said to be the son of Ares (Mars) or Hermes (Mercury) by Aphrodite (Venus).

38.18   *thoughts*.   Rime requires *thought*.

39. 5   *losse*.   Rime requires *lot*.

41.30–31   *I am the sonne of secret sweet conceite, &c.* The passage resembles Lord Oxford's poem, No. 40: see 47.12.

42. 8   *Lodge*.   Read *Lodg'd*.

24   *standes me op*. A good example of the ethical dative. *Op* is a misprint for *vp*.

28   (No. 37) *Brittons second dreame of Venus, &c.* Reprinted in *The Bower*, 1597, No. [22], D4ᵛ–E2ᵛ, with the following variants:

42.29   her] htr
    31   awakt] I vvakt
43. 3   but] bu
    8   to] ro
    9   My] Me
    14   Little] Littie
    15   sobt] sobd
    20   shadow] shadie
    22   thus] so
    33   humors] honors

44.10   thou] thon
    23   comfort] comfor
    27   still] full
    29   ouerthrow] onerthrow
45.10   assured] affured
    18   He] As
    22   armes] harme
    23   my] the
    24   rare] care
    29   fauor] sauour
    31   Caualiroes] Caualiers
46. 3   honour] bonour
    4   shippes] shippet
    8   in] on

The foregoing reading at 43.9 should be adopted. No. 37 is something like the first idyllium of Moschus.

42.30 *But sorrow thus.* The sense apparently requires *But
sorrowing thus.*

45.24–27 *O case most rare, &c.* Breton's fondness for this
"climbing figure" is commented on in the note to 30.16–21.

46.10 (No. 38) *A deuice of Diogenes Tubbe.* Reprinted in *The
Bower*, 1597, No. [23], E2ᵛ, with *but* (line 12) changed to *out* and
his (line 24) to *the*, and with the correction (line 16) *Diogenes.*
The subject-matter is sufficiently explained by these passages
from Diogenes Laertius (translated by C. D. Yonge, 1853, pp. 228,
230, 239): "They also relate that Alexander said that if he had
not been Alexander, he should have liked to be Diogenes";
"Once, while he was sitting in the sun in the Craneum, Alexander
was standing by, and said to him, 'Ask any favour you choose of
me.' And he replied, 'Cease to shade me from the sun!'"; "'I ...
am Diogenes the dog. . . . I fawn upon those who give me any-
thing, and bark at those who give me nothing, and bite the
rogues.'" Over his grave was placed a pillar (p. 246), "and on
that a dog in Parian marble." See also the *Greek Anthology*, II,
69, and Ausonius, ed. Rudolf Peiper (Leipzig, 1886), pp. 82–83.

46.29   (No. 39) *A Metaphor*. Reprinted, without variants, in *The Bower*, 1597, No. [24], E2ᵛ–E3. A copy of the first stanza only — untitled, unsigned, and with the single variant *makes* for *make* (47.3) — is preserved in MS. Rawlinson Poet. 85, fol. 114ᵛ.

30   *A Little fire*. The sense seems to require something like *A little puff*.

47.10   (No. 40) *Of the birth and bringing vp of desire*. Reprinted in *The Bower*, 1597, No. [25], E3, with the following variants:

47.11   WHen] *Only one upright stroke of the* H *is impressed*
14   was] waa *apparently*
15   then] t en
17   liked] lik'd (*sic*)
18   your] yuor

A copy in MS. Rawlinson Poet. 85, fol. 15, signed "Earle of Oxenforde," is reprinted in Grosart's edition of Oxford's work in *Miscellanies of the Fuller Worthies' Library*, IV (1872), 407–409, and offers the following variant readings:

47.11   pompe and prime] pryde and pompe
12   good] selfe
14   sore] Sad: with] and
15   had you] haddest thou: then] than
16   were you] wert thou: feares] teares
17   brought . . . a] lulled thee to thy: speach that] thoughtes
          wᶜʰ: men] one
18   your] thy
20   then] than: likes] loues
21   your] thy: fauour] Beauty
22   Who . . . your] Whome fyndest thou most thy
23   you] the
24   ten] A

It will be observed that the foregoing copy (like those in MS. Harleian 6910, fol. 145, MS. Harleian 7392, fols. 18ᵛ–19 [signed "Finis. LO. OX."], and MS. Additional 28635, fols. 85–85ᵛ) is exactly the same length as No. 40. Bishop Percy, however, in

Reliques of Ancient English Poetry, 1765 (ed. H. B. Wheatley, II [1887], 185–187), reprinted the poem with an initial and a final stanza which he found in a very late version (called "A Communication between Fancy and Desire") in Thomas Deloney's *The Garland of Good Will*, 1678 (ed. J. H. Dixon, pp. 105–106, Percy Society, 1851, vol. XXX):

> Come hither, shepherd's swain.
>   Sir, what do you require?
> I pray thee shew [to me] thy name?
>   My name is FOND DESIRE.
>
> Then, fond Desire, farewel!
>   Thou art no meat for me;
> I should be lothe [methinkes] to dwell
>   With such a one as thee.

The bracketed words are additions by Percy, who also changed *meat* to *mate*. Grosart accepts and reprints with Percy's alterations these two stanzas. Indeed it is remarkable that Percy's late and unauthoritative changes are copied by nearly all subsequent editors: they are adopted, for example, in John Hannah's *The Poems of Sir Walter Raleigh . . . and Other Courtly Poets*, 1875, 1892, pp. 142–143, and in J. T. Looney's strange edition of *The Poems of Edward de Vere Seventeenth Earl of Oxford*, 1921, pp. 10–11. But Percy's version in general and the two new stanzas in particular have (so far as I can see) no independent authority: the text of *The Bower* is certainly the more authoritative.

It should be observed that Oxford's authorship is vouched for by *The Arte of English Poesie*, 1589 (ed. Arber, pp. 215–216): "*Edvvard* Earle of Oxford a most noble and learned Gentleman made in this figure of responce an emble [*sic*] of desire otherwise called *Cupide* which from his excellencie and wit, I set downe some part of the verses, for example." Twelve short verses, corresponding to 47.11–16 are then quoted, the only changes being *Sad sighes* (line 14), *hadst thou* (line 15), and *wert thou* (line 16).

Oxford may have translated the poem from Desportes's
Amours de Diane, I. xxxvii (*Œuvres*, ed. Michiels, p. 28):

> Amour, quand fus-tu né?   Ce fut lors que la terre
> S'émaille de couleurs et les bois de verdeur.
> De qui fus-tu conçeu?   D'une puissante ardeur
> Qu' oisiveté lascive en soy-mesmes enserre.
>> Qui te donne pouvoir de nous faire la guerre?
> Les divers mouvemens d'esperance et de peur.
> Où te retires-tu?   Dedans un jeune cœur
> Que de cent mille traits cruellement j'enferre.
>> De qui fus-tu nourry?   D'une douce beauté,
> Qui eut pour la servir jeunesse et vanité.
> De quoy te repais-tu?   D'une belle lumiere.
>> Crains-tu point le pouvoir des ans et de la mort?
> Non; car, si quelque-fois je meurs par leur effort,
> Aussi-tost je retourne en ma forme premiere.

Or possibly he went directly to Desportes's original, a sonnet by
Panfilo Sassi, falsely attributed to Serafino Aquilano de' Cimi-
nelli (*Le Rime*, ed. Mario Menghini, I [1894], 221):

> Quando nascesti, Amor? — Quando la terra
>   Si revestí de verde e bel colore.
>   — De che sei generato? — D'un ardore
> Che ozio lascivo in se rachiude e serra.
> — Che ti produsse a farne tanta guerra?
>   — Calda speranza e gelido timore.
>   — Ove prima abitasti? — In gentil core
> Che sotto al mio valor presto s'atterra.
> — Che fu la to nutrice? — Giovenezza,
>   E le serve raccolte a lei dintorno
>   Legiadria, vanità, pompa e bellezza.
> — Di che ti pasce? — D'un guardar adorno.
>   — Pò contra te la morte e la vecchiezza?
>   — No, ch'io rinasco mille volte el giorno.

As many Elizabethan scholars know, the Italian sonnet was
translated by George Buchanan (*Poemata*, Amsterdam, 1687, p.
377) and was adapted by Thomas Watson (*The Hekatompathia*,

1582, sonnet 22; *Poems*, ed. Arber, p. 58). Buchanan's version is as follows:

> Quis puer ales? Amor. Genitor quis? Blandus ocelli
>   Ardor. Quo natus tempore? Vere novo.
> Quis locus excepit? Generosi pectoris aula.
>   Quae nutrix? primo flore juventa decens.
> Quo nutrit victu? Illecebris, vultuque venusto.
>   Qui comites? Levitas, otia, luxus, opes.
> Cur puero belli semper furiosa cupido?
>   Impellunt avidae spes, trepidique metus.
> Non metuit mortem? Non. Quare? Saepe renasci,
>   Saepe mori decies hunc brevis hora videt.

Watson admits that he has "inuerted the order of some verses of *Seraphine*, and added the two last of himselfe to make the rest to seeme the more patheticall." His adaptation follows:

> When werte thou borne sweet *Loue*? who was thy sire?
> When *Flora* first adorn'd *Dame Tellus* lap,
> Then sprung I forth from *Wanton hote desire*:
> Who was thy nurse to feede thee first with pap?
>   *Youth* first with tender hand bound vp my heade,
>   Then saide, with *Lookes* alone I should be fed;
> What maides had she attendant on her side,
> To playe, to singe, to rocke thee fast a sleepe?
> *Vaine Nicenesse, Beautie Faire*, and *Pompeous Pride*;
> By stealth when further age on thee did creepe;
>   Where didst thou make thy chiefe abiding place?
>   In *Willing Hartes*, which were of gentle race;
> What is't wherewith thou wagest warres with me?
> *Feare* colde as Ise, and *Hope* as hote as fire;
> And can not age or death make end of thee?
> No, no, my dying life still makes retire;
>   Why then sweete *Loue* take pittie on my paine,
>   Which often dye, and oft reuiue againe.

Breton himself apparently had in mind the verses of "Serafino," Watson, or Desportes when in *The Wil of Wit*, ca. 1582 (1599 edition, Grosart's Breton, II, *c*, 11–12), he wrote "A Song

betweene Wit and Will," which in part (omitting the speech-tags)
runs thus:

> What art thou, Will?
> A babe of natures brood.
> Who was thy syre?
> Sweet lust, as lovers say.
> Thy mother who?
> Wild lustie wanton blood.
> When wert thou borne?
> In merrie moneth of May.
> And where brought up?
> In schoole of little skill,
> What learndst thou there?
> Love is my Lesson still.

See also the note to 41.30–31.

47.26   (No. 41) *A pleasant Sonet.* Reprinted in *The Bower*,
1597, No. [26], E3–E3ᵛ, with the following variants:

47.35   may] might
48. 2   Vermelion] Vermilion
   17   when] whence
   24   dost] doest

A longer and a better copy of the poem will be found in MS. Harleian 7392, fols. 64ᵛ–65. It varies as follows:

47.26   *Title om.*
   32   winnest] wynst
   34   eyes] eyen
48. 2   Vermelion] vermylion
   3   Saint] Queene: thou] yow
   4   *MS. adds:*

> I wyll forgett those paps so swanny whyte
> I wyll forget those rare lyke brestes of thyne
>   I wyll forgett thou art my cheef delyghte.
> I wyll forgett thou art my mystres Shee
> I wyll forgett the sweetst that ere I see.
>
>   I wyll forgett where thou dost styll abyde

48. 5   approch] approachd: seemely] present
    8   stainst] staynest
    10   feature is] features not
    12   that] for: not] none
    14   fairest] fayrst
    17   when] whence
    18   eate] care
    19   to ³] or
    25   *MS. adds:*

    Only yowr Serv:
    though not ŷ only Serv:
    FINIS. I Ed.

All but three lines of No. 41 begin "I will forget," a mechanical repetition characteristic of Breton. For example, in *I Would And Would not*, 1614, nearly every stanza begins "I would" or "And yet I would not." The manuscript copy, however, is apparently signed "I Ed." (a signature found on fols. 65ᵛ and 72ᵛ, while "Ioh Ed." and "I E" occur on fols. 67 and 72ᵛ).

47.32   *thou winnest the golden ball.* That is, for beauty, as Venus won the golden apple by the judgment of Paris.

48. 3   *but thou.* Grammar and rime demand *but you.*

    4, 6   *fine, wide.* This faulty rime is caused by the omission of the lines found in the manuscript.

    26   (No. 42) *Another sweete Sonet.* Reprinted in *The Bower*, 1597, No. [27], E3ᵛ–E4, with the following variants:

48.26   Another] Auother
    30   to] ro *apparently*
    31   am] *The* m *is inverted*
    32   lo] so
49. 2   secke] seekes

49.12   (No. 43) *A Poem.* Reprinted in *The Bower*, 1597, No. [28], E4, with *and* (line 14) misprinted *aud.* Hopton, whose name is spelled in acrostic-form, is evidently the Anne Hopton mentioned in the list of maids of honor to whom in 1588/9 the queen gave gifts of gilt plate (John Nichols, *The Progresses and Public Processions of Queen Elizabeth*, III [1823], 20). The daughter of Sir Owen Hopton, lieutenant of the Tower, she married Henry Wentworth, third Baron Wentworth, of Nettlestead (1558–1593), and, after his death, William Pope, first Earl of Downe. For a portrait of Lady Wentworth and her three children, see the reproduction in *The Third Annual Volume of the Walpole Society*, 1914, plate XI.

49.19   (No. 44) *A Sonet.* Reprinted in *The Bower*, 1597, No. [29], E4–E4ᵛ, with *vntill* (line 23) misprinted *vntitil* and *herselfe* ² (50.6) *her elfe.*

28   *in her silent speaking.* One would expect *silence*, but it is hardly worth while to attempt to emend such frigid, conceited poems as this.

50. 7   *two sonnes. Two suns* is an odd figure to apply to the breasts.

9   (No. 45) *Another fine Sonet.* Reprinted in *The Bower*, 1597, No. [30], E4ᵛ, with *truth deserue* (line 16) changed to *truerh deserues.* The last word should be the adopted reading. Proverbs, slightly changed from their usual form, make up the bulk of the poem.

28   (No. 46) *A Pastorall.* Reprinted, without variants, in *The Bower*, 1597, No. [31], E4ᵛ–F1. It has been pointed out by Norman Ault (*Elizabethan Lyrics*, 1925, pp. 507, 510) that Thomas Heywood lavishly borrows from this poem in *The Fair Maid of the Exchange*, 1607 (*Dramatic Works*, ed. Pearson, II, 33), where Frank Golding sings:

> Ye little birds that sit and sing
> Amidst the shady valleyes,
> And see how *Phillis* sweetly walkes
> Within her Garden alleyes;
> Goe pretty birds about her bowre,
> Sing pretty birds she may not lowre,
> Ah me, me thinkes I see her frowne,
>   Ye pretty wantons warble.

Goe tell her through your chirping bils,
As you by me are bidden,
To her is onely knowne my love,
Which from the world is hidden:
Goe pretty birds and tell her so,
See that your notes straine not too low,
For still me thinkes I see her frowne,
　　Ye pretty wantons warble.

Goe tune your voices harmony,
And sing I am her Lover;
Straine lowde and sweet, that every note,
With sweet content may move her:
And she that hath the sweetest voyce,
Tell her I will not change my choyce,
Yet still me thinkes I see her frowne,
　　Ye pretty wantons warble.

O fly, make haste, see, see, she falles
Into a pretty slumber,
Sing round about her rosie bed
That waking she may wonder,
Say to her, tis her lover true,
That sendeth love to you, to you:
And when you heare her kind reply,
Returne with pleasant warblings.

"Heywood's" lyric is sung by Bellafront in Thomas Dekker's *The Honest Whore*, II. i (1604), and apparently by the sixth gossip in Samuel Rowlands's *A Whole Crew of Kind Gossips*, 1609. It reappeared in revised and lengthened form in *The Nightingale*, 1742, pp. 119–120.

51. 8 (No. 47) *Coridons supplication to Phillis.* Reprinted in *The Bower*, 1597, No. [32], F1, with the following variants:

51.17　presumed] presum'd [*sic*]
　19　consumed] consum'd [*sic*]
　27　grunnt] graunt
　31　dost] doest
52. 2　allowed] allowde
　3　disdained] disdainde

A copy, entitled "Choridons supplication," in MS. Additional 34064, fols. 10–10ᵛ, has the following variants:

51.17   so] to: presumed] presumde
   19   consumed] consumde
   25   bruise] browse
   26   pricke] picke
   27   grunnt] graunt
   34   ordained] ordeynde
52. 2   yet allowed] ytt allowde
    3   disdained] disdainde
    7   behoue] behoofe
    8   Coridon] Choridon: consent] content
   10   content] consent

The foregoing readings at 51.25, 26, 27, 52.8 (*content*), 10 should be adopted. From the 1597 edition the poem passed into *England's Helicon*, 1600, H4–H4ᵛ, with the signature of "N. Breton."

   52.12   (No. 48) *A Sonet*. Reprinted in *The Bower*, 1597, No. [33], F1–F1ᵛ, with the following variants:

52.18   learne] leat ne *apparently*
   22   beame] line
53.15   loue] liue

Other versions of this popular, but worthless, poem will be found in *The Phoenix Nest*, 1593, K4–K4ᵛ; in William Barley's *A newv Booke of Tabliture, Containing sundrie easie and familiar Instructions*, 1596, A4ᵛ (cf. E. H. Fellowes, *English Madrigal Verse*, pp. 312–313); in *A Poetical Rhapsody*, 1602–1621 (ed. Rollins, I [1931], 223); in *Wits Recreations*, 1641, T1ᵛ, 1645, S5ᵛ (other editions appeared in 1650, 1654, 1663, etc.); in John Cotgrave's *Wits Interpreter, The English Parnassus*, 1655, G7ᵛ–G8 (also 1662, 1671); in *Le Prince d'Amour*, 1660, pp. 131–132; and in MS. Additional 15227, fols. 84ᵛ–85, MS. Rawlinson Poet. 117, fols. 161, 168ᵛ, MS. Additional 22118, fol. 34. John Hannah accepted Raleigh as the author (*The Poems of Sir Walter Raleigh*, etc., 1875, 1892, pp. 15–16), and is followed by Raleigh's most recent (1929) editor, Agnes

M. C. Latham, p. 38. For fuller details see my edition of *The Phoenix Nest*, pp. 173–178.

53. 6 (No. 49) *A Louers complaint*. Reprinted, without variants, in *The Bower*, 1597, No. [34], F1ᵛ–F2. Another copy is preserved in MS. Harleian 7392, fol. 71ᵛ, varying as follows:

53. 6   *Title om.*
    12   And can y̆ same descry [cf. 53.8]
    13   thereof he] he therof
    16   If] and
    19   Who's] Who is
    20   Turrets] Tower
    21   that] and
    23   Who's] Who is
    25   So deare to] or who will
    26   but] save
    29   would] will: such] the
    30   but] save
    31   and] or
54. 5   And . . . to] In fine I here do

No. 49 is a ballad — perhaps one that Richard Jones issued in broadside-form before 1591.

54. 9 (No. 50) *A Shepheards dreame*. Reprinted in *The Bower*, 1597, No. [35], F2–F2ᵛ, with each two short lines printed as one long line, with *before* (54.25) misprinted apparently as *hefore*, and with the correct reading *good* at 55.11. An untitled copy in MS. Additional 34064, fols. 11ᵛ–12, varies as follows:

54. 18   whopt] whoopte
    20   sore] so
55. 10   stand] staie

Probably from the 1597 edition the poem made its way into *England's Helicon*, 1600, K3ᵛ–K4, where it is signed "N. Breton."

55. 16 (No. 51) *A pleasant sweet song*. Reprinted in *The Bower*, 1597, No. [36], F2ᵛ, *As* (line 24) changed to *And*, *rise* (line 24) misprinted as apparently *tise*, *the* (line 25) substituted for *a*. The

poem is a greatly condensed version of the Earl of Surrey's "How no age is content with his own estate, & how the age of children is the happiest, if they had skill to vnderstand it" (Tottel's *Miscellany*, No. 33), which begins,

> Layd in my quiét bed, in study as I were,
>   I saw within my troubled head, a heape of thoughtes appere:
> And euery thought did shew so liuely in myne eyes,
>   That now I sighed, & thē I smilde, as cause of thought doth ryse.

For further details see my edition of Tottel's *Miscellany*, II, 157–158.

56.10   (No. 52) *A Sonet of Time and Pleasure*. Reprinted in *The Bower*, 1597, No. [37], F3, with *short the* (line 11) misprinted *shott the*. An untitled copy in MS. Additional 34064, fol. 13ᵛ, has the following variants:

56.12   Pleasures] pleasure
   26   And in the sweete of loues desired lappe
   30   do] dothe

57. 2   (No. 53) *Of a Louer in dispaire*. Reprinted, without variants, in *The Bower*, 1597, No. [38], F3.

11   (No. 54) *A Sonet of faire womens ficklenesse in loue*. Reprinted in *The Bower*, 1597, No. [39], F3ᵛ, with *that* (line 14) changed to *if*. A copy in MS. Rawlinson Poet. 85, fol. 16, entitled "Fayre Fooles" and signed "Earle of Oxenforde," is printed in Grosart's edition of Oxford's works in *Miscellanies of the Fuller Worthies' Library*, IV (1872), 420–421, with the following variants:

57.13   would] could
   15   wonder] meruayle
   17   firme these] frayll those
   18   laugh] muse
   19   their] the
   20   Venus] Phœbus: cleaue] flee
   21   vile] willd

57.23   his] the
  24   go] flye
  25   If] Yet: faine] fawne
  26   can displease] else cañ please
  27   still vnto our] to our lure with
  28   wits] wiles
  29   fancies] fancye
  30   dolt] foole

At least the foregoing readings at 57.17, 21, 28 should be adopted.

The Rawlinson copy was likewise printed by Sir Egerton Brydges and Joseph Haslewood in their edition of *England's Helicon*, 1812, p. xxvi; by John Hannah in *The Poems of Sir Walter Raleigh*, 1875, 1892, pp. 143–144; and by J. T. Looney in *The Poems of Edward de Vere Seventeenth Earl of Oxford*, 1921, p. 37: The first appearance of No. 54 in print seems to have been in William Byrd's *Psalmes, Sonets, & Songs of Sadnes and Pietie*, 1588, No. 17 (the words are reprinted in Brydges's *Censura Literaria*, II [1815], 114, and in E. H. Fellowes's *English Madrigal Verse*, 1920, p. 40), where the verses are considerably different, and where the music to which they were sung is included. This version is reprinted below (from Fellowes), since many of the lines in *The Bower* are unintelligible:

> If women could be fair and never fond,
>   Or that their beauty might continue still,
> I would not marvel though they made men bond
>   By service long to purchase their goodwill;
> But when I see how frail these creatures are
> I laugh that men forget themselves so far.
>
> To mark what choice they make, and how they change;
>   How, leaving best, the worst they choose out still;
> And how, like haggards wild, about they range,
>   Scorning after reason to follow will:
> Who would not shake such buzzards from the fist,
> And let them fly (fair fools) which way they list?

Yet for our sport we fawn and flatter both,
    To pass the time when nothing else can please,
And train them on to yield by subtle oath
    The sweet content that gives such humour ease.
And then we say, when we their follies try,
To play with fools, O what a fool was I.

Considerably changed, also, is the copy that surprizing plagia-rist, Samuel Pick, included as his own work in *Festum Voluptatis; Or, The Banquet of Pleasure*, 1639, C3–C3ᵛ:

57.11   *Title changed to* An invective against Women
    13   would] could
    15   bond] bound
    16   seruice] serving
    17   firme] fraile
    19   their] the
    20   Venus] Phœbus: cleaue] change
    21   vile] wild
    23   his] the
    25   If] Yet: disport] their sport: faine] fawne
    26   can displease] else can please
    27   still vnto] to our lure by
    28   their wits] our wills
    29   fancies] fancy

57.31   (No. 55) *Of the foure Elements*. Reprinted in *The Bower*, 1597, No. [40], F3ᵛ–F4, with the following variants:

57.31   Elements] Elemenes
58.10   Fire] the
    13   thy flowers not] not thy Flowers

A copy, entitled "Quatuor elementa," in MS. Additional 34064, fol. 19ᵛ, has the following variants:

58. 2   spirit] spritt
    8   whote] hott
    17   slaie] slaine (?):   once] one
    21   Oh] ah: my] *Om.*

58.22   do] to
   23   power] powres
   27   floweth] flowthe
   28   worde] world

The foregoing reading (*spritt*, or *sprite*) at 58.2 should be adopted. Many more variants will be found in the untitled copies preserved in MS. Harleian 6910, fols. 148ᵛ–149 (*A*), and MS. Harleian 7392, fol. 68ᵛ (*B*):

57.32   do] doth *AB*
   33   heauie] gazing *A*
58. 2   spirit] spright *AB*
    6   sore I] I do *AB*
    7   Earth, her flowers do] Earth [Earthes *B*] fayer flowers doth [do *B*] *AB*
    8   The fire with heat enflames the frozen mynd *A*, The ffyre so hot, enflames my [*marginal note* the] frozen mynde *B*
    9   white] Heate *B*
   11   needes] all *B*
   14   a colde] ycoulde *B*
   16   Or, or] Oh, oh *AB*
   17   once] now *A*, ôh *B*
   21   Oh] Ah *AB*:   my . . . appalleth] panting harts apaleth *AB*
   23   power] powers *A*
   25   the] is *B*
   26   cole and bauen] flame and furie *AB*
   27   ebth] ebbs *AB*
   28   in a worde] wᵗʰin a World *B*
   29   heart hath] harts haue *AB*:   rest] Joyes *A*

The foregoing readings at 58.9, 16 should perhaps be adopted. Presumably from a manuscript John Fry printed another version (beginning, "The Ayre wᵗʰ sweetes my sences doth delight") in *Pieces of Ancient Poetry, from Unpublished Manuscripts and Scarce Books*, 1814, pp. 8–9. No. 55 bears every sign of Breton's authorship.

58.30   (No. 56) *Brittons farewell to Hope.* Reprinted in *The Bower*, 1597, No. [41], F4–F4ᵛ, with the following variants:

59.17   becke] backe
   20   faire] faite
   21   that] the
   25   but] hut
   29   *is followed by a large type-ornament*

No. 56 resembles Breton's acknowledged work in every particular.

59.29   *FINIS. N. B. Gent.* This signature was, in my opinion, intended by Jones to apply to the entire *Bower*, not merely to
No. 56.

INDEXES

INDEX OF FIRST LINES

INDEX OF NAMES AND TITLES

References are to pages of the Introduction and the Notes. Nicholas Breton and *The Bower* are mentioned on nearly every page, and are not entered in this Index.